T3-BWY-501

Life Teachings:
Raising a Child

Life Teachings: Raising a Child

Jeanie Davis Pullen

Yellow House Productions
St. Paul, Minnesota

First printing.

Yellow House Productions, P.O. Box 270307, St. Paul, MN 55127
    www.YellowHouseProductions.com

Book design by Dorie McClelland, Spring Type & Design

Publisher's Cataloging-in-Publication
(Provided by Quality Books, Inc.)

    Pullen, Jeanie Davis
        Life teachings : raising a child / Jeanie Davis Pullen — 1st ed.
        p.cm.

        1. Child rearing. 2. Child psychology. 3. Moral development.
    4. Parenting   I. Title.

    HQ772.P85 1999   649.7
                                              QB199-677

    ISBN: 0-9672660-0-9

to Lara and Julie

Contents

The first twenty years of my life were spent in Kentucky, and I remember adults from the family and community talking on the porch on warm, lazy afternoons and into the evenings. I remember that many important matters were settled and learned about in that easy, musing fashion. I heard much wisdom transferred on that childhood porch.

The porch musings were filled with wisdom based upon someone's experiences and knowledge. That person did not need to be an expert. The wisdom came in several layers and I think that was some of the value. There were many facets of the porch musings and each who heard the talking took a little more from the experience than just the topic at hand. So, too, *Life Teachings: Raising a Child*—there is more here than meets the eye. Using your own intellect and your experiences, you will find information in each small chapter that goes beyond the topic at hand.

Like the adults in the rockers on the porch of my childhood, I am not an expert. Instead, I am an educator who has given many talks over the years. My most requested talks have been about child raising, communications, and crafting growth paths in education and life. And, I have raised two daughters who are highly educated and successful in their lives and careers. You'll read about them in *Life Teachings: Raising a Child.*

I invite you to pull up a rocker and have some iced tea as we muse together over the crucial matter of forming a foundation for a child. The introduction tells you of the philosophy that guided my childraising. You'll find that important, for it sets the scene. Then, we get into the stories that tell you how the philosophy played. Perhaps in our porch musings, you will find some wisdom here, something that will be of use to you.

Introduction

In our lives, people and experiences have formed who we are at this moment. From the time we are born until we die, people and experiences show us a way to conduct our lives. Our first encounter with people and experiences is, of course, through our parents and involved family members. They arrange the experiences that create the foundation of who we will become as we get older. Through their selections, our parents show us what to value, how to behave, and how to interact with other people. Sometimes the selections that our parents make are conscious choices and sometimes the choices are not conscious. Regardless, it is through our parents and involved family members that we first see a way to conduct our lives.

Human instincts that are present when we are born push us into questioning why one particular way of life is presented to us and not another. Very early in childhood, a child asks many "why" questions of parents. This questioning can continue for the rest of one's life.

Once we begin asking questions of our environment, our people, and our experiences, we begin the process of choosing the way of life that will be ours. Since we never really cease in our involvement with people and experiences, we are constantly hearing, seeing, and doing new experiences. And, each of the new experiences and people validate, refine, and perhaps even redesign what we believe is the best way of life for us.

Our selection of the best approach to life comes from many sources. Regardless of whether we are rich or poor, school educated or not, we all approach the selection in basically the same way. We observe what is in our field of vision- people and experiences. We observe people's behavior as they interact with each other and how they act when we see them alone. We observe whether a person's words match behavior, and we observe how our supervisors at work conduct themselves. We observe our own behaviors, our emotions in situations and interactions, and our health and energy levels. We read of people and their experiences, we watch television, we go to the movies, we go to school, and we go to church. Daily, through people and experiences, we build our understanding of what is fair and proper as we hone the way of life that we like. Throughout our adult lives, we continually create our personal approach to life as we adjust, enhance, or scrap the childhood foundation we received.

We create our approach to life through the choices we make, whether conscious or unconscious. If we are aware of the choices we have, we realize that we have a pretty heady decision in the matter and, further, we know that we can change ourselves if we do not like who we have crafted.

Life Teachings: Raising a Child tells how a childhood

foundation was created for my two daughters. My husband and I consciously chose the experiences and values that would form the foundation upon which the girls would later build. *Life Teachings: Raising a Child* is a collection of family stories that illustrate how we shaped the traits and skills that we wanted our daughters to possess by the time they were young adults. As you read this book, you will see that life teachings other than the obviously mentioned ones are being transferred. So it is with life. As you read my stories, know that if your childhood stories were written and outsiders read them, then they also would see the messages that you the parent transferred or you the child received. Regardless of whether or not the parent or child was aware of the transfer, the transfer did occur.

If you are a parent, *Life Teachings: Raising a Child* suggests that you be purposeful and conscious of the way you interact with your children, particularly when they are young. You remember how your own parents interacted with you. You remember many things about your parents. Your child is watching you and taking in your messages, too. Yes, you are tired and overworked, but your parents were too. Choices are made each day; and it is good to have a conscious input into your interactions.

You will see threads woven through the stories as I tell you of the interactions in my family.

The threads support a template or game plan that guided our child raising. You have a template, too; sometimes templates are apparent only after the child-raising part is over. This book suggests that if you form the game plan first, the carrying out is more purposeful and more likely to occur.

As you read, you may find useful life information, even if you have no children. The book depicts a way of life that honors the fact that we are always growing ourselves, long after the official childhood is over. After our childhood, we become the teacher as well as the student.

You may find yourself reading from several perspectives. You may examine the template and the supporting stories in relationship to your own childhood. You may read from a parent's viewpoint, whether you have a child now or one is in your plans. You may consider the template and see where you yourself are today. Or, you may take the basic template and make changes or additions to form one that would suit you, knowing that you continue to create yourself.

I have spoken to many groups of people about the creation of one's approach to life, using some of the same stories that you will read. While I regularly hear from several people immediately after each talk, I also often hear from people several days later. Each of the people tells me the same thing. They say that the information from it had a great impact on their lives. Some had children and some did not, but each said that the information meant something powerful to them personally, and in some cases was life changing for them.

Over the years, many people have requested that I write about the importance and responsibility of an individual determining and creating a personal way of life. Using family child-raising stories for illustration, I have written this book.

Life Teachings: Raising a Child can remind us of a higher path of life and one that is quite doable, if we are mindful and conscious of our choices.

1 *One day, I was listening to my adult children...*

I listened to Lara and Julie talk easily and excitedly with each other about their scientific ideas and philosophical thoughts. These were my daughters, now in their late twenties. I looked at the ocean at our feet and my thoughts spun as I wondered how children develop to this point? How do they become functioning, confident, happy adults who contribute positively to society? How does it all happen? Was it luck and the brashness and ignorance of their parents' youth, or was there something else at work? I watched and heard the quickness and care with which Lara and Julie exchanged ideas and later, as they instructed me as to what we were seeing in the tidepools of the Oregon coast, I began to silently muse about what was in front of me.

Both girls are happy with themselves and their worlds. They are respectful of themselves and other people, and successful in both their personal and work worlds. The oldest, Lara, has completed a Ph.D. in immunology, and Julie is finishing a Ph.D. in physical oceanography. In addition to their successful schooling, each daughter is the kind of person that one likes being around, indeed, would seek to be around. Each is kind, intelligent, with a sense of humor and a solid feel for fairness in their interactions. Each is the kind of child that a parent dreams will emerge from their efforts at raising a child.

As I watched Lara and Julie play with their ideas that day in Oregon, I realized that it was all in front of me. But what was I seeing? I knew that what I was seeing gave me great pleasure, but I couldn't help wondering just how the product took this shape. What was the process, and what assistance did the product have in its shaping?

During most of the three-hour return flight to Minnesota, I continued to question myself as I sorted things out. I understood that children come into the world with many wonderful skills and abilities. Acknowledging this, I soon put my attention to what could happen consistently in the home to encourage the child to grow well and learn positively from her/his experiences. I began to examine Lara and Julie's upbringing. I reached further and further into my past and into the girls' early lives for insight.

After awhile, I smiled and reached for a pencil and the margins of the airline's magazine. I had some thoughts, perhaps even answers. I knew what I would tell the girls when they asked for specifics about raising their own children. I also knew what I would say to the next parents who sought specifics of me saying, "We have this child. We want to do a good job of raising him, but how do we do it? What do you suggest?" I knew what I would say to the young parents who came proudly and a little shyly to me and said, "We are expecting a child. How do we raise our little one? We know the traits that we want for our child, but how can we encourage them? What can we do? We want our child to be...."

2 *I prepared for my life as a parent.*

In April 1967, I became pregnant with Lara, the first of our two daughters. Julie was born in 1969. I did not know what motherhood would mean to me, but, according to my nature, I looked forward, with great curiosity, wonderment, and interest, to what I could learn from the experience.

Very early in the pregnancy, I decided that motherhood meant that I was to guide my child's preparation for life. While this is quite simple and nothing new, the next step was not so simple. I had to determine what "preparation for life" meant to me. It seemed reasonable to assume that I was responsible for more than protecting her physical safety. I needed to provide shelter, food, and clothing and to see her through her forming years and into young adulthood. I was responsible for explaining and showing her tools of life, the life lessons that I thought were important and that I knew worked well based on what I had experienced during my life and the things that I had sought to understand.

In order to do motherhood well, I felt that I needed to look twenty years in the future to examine what kind of adult I wanted my baby to become. I certainly did not want to determine what she would do with her life. However, I did want to know what kind of life equipment would be the most helpful and the least restrictive as she made her way. I concentrated only on the abstract, for she would need to create the details of her own life.

I thought of many life traits that I wanted for my daughter. For each trait, I imagined twenty years into the future to see the implications. From that viewpoint, if any life trait seemed needlessly restrictive or unimportant, I dropped it or adjusted it. Many were rejected. If a trait were kept on the list, I would move to the next step of examining how the life trait could be taught in forming the child. The list of life traits would become a template to guide me in the raising of my daughter.

The template I sought would function as does a warm coat for Minnesota winters. A warm coat is necessary for the child to feel capable in the very cold environment. Without the coat, she would not successfully interact with the Minnesota cold. The cold would slow her actions and thoughts and she would focus her attention on the physical need to keep her body warm. If I formed it well, the template would act like the coat. Not only would it equip her for her physical environment and experiences, it would afford her the comfort to proceed with self-confidence and wisdom as she moved forward in her world.

There was a second requirement for the template. I needed to consistently live it. If the life traits were for life, then they had to be for me, too. To have it otherwise was not fair, and I knew that fair play would be an item on the template.

Eventually, I formed a mental template that would guide

my motherhood. Each attribute was general, with large amounts of developing room to accommodate my own growth and situations that could occur in my daughter's life. I decided that after the twenty years had passed, and she was a young adult, the following traits would be enormously helpful to her. This, then, became my template.

In twenty years, I wanted my daughter to:
be happy,
trust her own counsel,
have a strong element of care and fair play for herself and
    others,
have no guilt,
appreciate the role that people play in her life,
be able to thank people,
be able to see and comment on the good in herself and in
    others,
have a light in her eye,
be able to pull information from her environment,
have a sense of wonderment,
understand that there is more to this life than the physical,
be gracious,
be loving to the people who matter most to her,
be able to see beauty in everyday things,
appreciate nature's role in life,

have a love of words,
be confident,
have wisdom, and
communicate well.

Although the list may appear daunting, it did not seem so to me. The items on the list were very important to me. The list was never written down. I made the list a part of me. I wanted to know the template so thoroughly that it would be constantly available to me. I was comfortable with the list, for it fit me. And it seemed to carry nothing that would cripple, but only help, my daughter in her life.

In some ways, my template was a mission plan, a game plan. Next, I needed to figure out what the supporting pieces would be and how they could be consistently delivered and lived. I expected the supporting pieces to exert an influence that I would recognize in Lara and Julie's independent lives. Future behaviors and events would become yardsticks to measure the effectiveness of the template.

Since I prize freedom and independence for myself, I knew that the template would be delivered with few rules and regula-tions. That was part of the fair play, for I did not like many rules and regulations in my own life and I could not impose on my daughter something that would be so very hard for me. Besides, I felt the game plan could be delivered without many restrictions.

As I prepared for my life as a mother, I gave close attention to life situations around me that particularly involved children and their parents. I noticed parents and their children at the grocery, at the doctor's office, and at social gatherings. I saw child behaviors and child-parent interactions that I liked, and I saw many that I didn't like. I noticed that I favored the interactions and behaviors that demonstrated respect-respect for self, for others, and for the environment. I concluded that very few behaviors and interactions just happened; instead, they were guided, valued, and rewarded by someone, most likely a parent/guardian, or two.

I began to see a plan of action for situations in which my child and I would be involved. The plan would have respect at its core-my respect for the growing child, and the child's respect for herself, her parents, the environment, and other people. I was ready for the birth of my child and eager to see how the template played.

3 *I realized that respect was a huge over-arching theme.*

In my life, I usually seek the big picture in matters and issues and this one was clear to me. I realized that respect was a huge over-arching theme in my life and on the template. If I could convey the importance of respect to my child and then help the child live in a respectful way, then I could feel comfortable with having given her a useful approach to life. I knew that by respect, I meant respect for herself and her own growth, for others and their growth, and for her small and large environments.

It was natural that I would value respect and that it would show up so clearly in my adult-to-be template. For many years, I have believed that we come to this earth for experiences. That is what life is about. How we approach and what we learn from each experience mold our lives and influence each future experience. People, places, environments, and situations compose experiences. They are valuable and deserve respect.

Increasingly, I found my thoughts replacing the noun respect with the adjective respectful. It seemed to me that respect was a static end product-a place where one could put a period. Respectful, on the other hand, seemed like an action approach.

So, the assignment became to find ways that one can interact with self, other people, environments small and large, circumstances and situations, in a respectful manner.

4 *As soon as Lara was born, I began acquainting her with the world she had entered.*

I mainly talked about process. I spoke about how things are done and why.

Lara and Julie were born at a time when babies did not stay in the hospital room with the mother, so I only saw them when they were brought for nursing or bathing. Most of my attention was taken with learning the proper way to bathe a baby, how best to nurse, and trying to remember the advice that the caring nurse was giving to me.

Once I got home from the hospital, Michael and I began regular talking to the baby. We both believed that the baby needed to know what was going on and why. We further believed that the baby could hear and understand on an important level, and that hearing and understanding occurred any time the child's eyes were open. We did not talk baby talk. We spoke as we would to a person visiting us from another culture or country. That person would have sense but not know the specifics of the environment in which he was visiting. We explained things.

During the first year, the explaining involved activities, like the steps of changing the diaper, running the bath water, warming the milk bottle, washing the clothes. Nearly everything has a process to it and thus steps to talk through. This talking was done out loud and one-on-one, directed at the child. Before she was turning over by herself, Lara was placed in a carrier on the kitchen counter by the sink. As I washed dishes and cooked a meal, I talked the steps out loud. As plans were made for outings, anything and everything was talked softly, one-to-one. This talking out loud continued with new processes until each girl was nearly three. As they became more mobile, they would wander around on the floor as we spoke out loud to them.

By age three, I noticed that Lara was talking to Julie in this fashion, explaining the ropes to her. And, Julie, in her turn, explained things to her dolls and stuffed animals. Michael and I were always charmed as we heard these exchanges.

When I was in elementary school learning math concepts, I would sometimes become stuck with a new process. My daddy always encouraged me to talk the steps out loud as I went through them. "Listen to what you are saying as you sort it out," he said to me. Quite often, hearing myself say the process out loud helped me figure it out. Logic, a pattern, or a solution often became apparent. While I most remember Daddy reminding me during math woes, he expected me to say out loud what I knew about problems in general, and listen to what I was saying. I realize now that he was teaching me to analyze. At the time, I just knew that verbalizing each step helped me see. Through their elementary and secondary schooling, Lara and Julie often talked the steps out loud when they confronted a homework problem.

While I am a strong believer in talking, I remember a time when it was best for me not to talk. We had just moved to Maryland from California. In California, Lara would have been in kindergarten, but in Maryland, she would be in first grade. We left California before the start of school, drove across the United States, and arrived in Maryland nearly two weeks after school had started.

As Lara and I walked the three short blocks to the school, she and I held hands and talked brightly. But as we approached the sidewalk to Crofton Woods Elementary, Lara said "Mama, I'm so scared." After a two- or three-second pause, and before I could collect myself enough to say comforting words of logic, she added staunchly, "But, I know that by the time today is over and you come to collect me, I will have made some friends, and will know my teacher, and will be happy to be in first grade." I squeezed her hand in agreement.

In a sincere statement, my little girl had logically comforted herself as well as I could have. Lara's statement to herself and me helped me immensely for I was having a very difficult time holding back tears as my little one took the big step of starting school. We found her classroom, and the teacher introduced herself to Lara and began helping her know the environment. At this point, the most I could do was ask the teacher in a choked voice to please take good care of my little girl. She assured me that she would. On my walk back home, I was impressed by the fact that my not answering Lara's fears too quickly had allowed her to talk out loud to herself with logic. We both would have said the same kind of words, but the words were stronger coming from her, for she could hear her own words and understand her own logic.

Years later, one of my high school students, a senior boy, stayed after class one day and told me that matters had gotten so rough living with his father, that he was leaving home and staying with a friend. He wanted me to know. I was so very touched with this young man's sadness that I wasn't sure how to express my concern and care for him. In the second I was collecting my thoughts, he filled in the space by taking my hand. "Don't worry about me, Jeanie, for I am in good hands. I'm going to be fine. And I will let you know regularly how I am and where I am. Don't worry." I touched his face while I nodded and gave him a hug. My student had said all that I would have said. I again learned that there are poignant moments when talking is not needed.

5 *Young children believe what parents say to them.*

As I observed parents interacting with their children, I saw how powerfully words can hurt and scar. Young children believe what parents say to them, particularly if the same comments are repeated. One afternoon, in the grocery, I watched as a mother, in her attempts to discipline her child, told him that he was always a troublemaker. No wonder people didn't like him. The police would likely be talking to him soon. In essence, his mama was telling him he was no good. Her words were forming how he saw himself. As I heard hurtful words being said to children, I remembered two simple stories from my own childhood.

When my daddy was a young boy, he and his large family lived on a tobacco farm in Kentucky. Farming is hard work for every family member. One spring night after chores were done, Daddy and his mother were outside together. His mother was in a rocking chair, a large pan in her lap, shelling peas for the next day's cooking. Daddy was sprawled on the ground, looking up at the dark sky, filled with billions of stars. "Mama, when I grow up, I'm going to have a dollar for every star in the sky." His mother was tired after a full day of work and she didn't believe that he would ever have that much money—he couldn't even finish his daily chores without constant reminding. Making money required work and that boy of hers was not a proven worker yet. She could have said any of these things to this dreamer, but instead she waited for him to continue. "And, Mama, I am going to give you a whole lot of that money!" " I know you will, Gabe, for you are a good, kind boy. You always have been. I know you will take care of your Mama." The boy was pleased with her words and went on with his thoughts. That night, his mama had been tired and likely not in the mood for outlandish, impossible foolishness. But she knew that the two of them were not talking about reality but about dreams. In her wisdom, she did not want to sully soft, musing dream talk with reality when it was not necessary.

Daddy told this story several times during my childhood, but it took me awhile to notice that the story was never changed. It occurred to me that with the perspective of time, Daddy could say that his mama knew he was not a worker, or that money for every star is impossible, but those words were never said. The story remained intact, with no jesting laughter attached. And, the story was never interpreted for us children. The story stood along with whatever message we took from it. The son, my daddy, grew up and earned a large amount of money, and took very good care of his mama. I wonder if the outcome would have been different if his mama had felt a responsibility to respond to her son with a large amount of reality. Instead, Mama ignored the reality of his slow work and the impossibility of having a dollar for every star, and concentrated only on a piece of reality that fit the dream-her son was good and kind. By emphasizing the positive reality only, she let the dream stand. And, what a difference her action made.

Later in my own childhood, my maternal grandmother performed a similar deed for me. As a young teenager, I was tall and had very long, slender feet. I could not buy shoes off the rack in our small town. Instead, one of the local shoe store owners selected several pairs of shoes at market for me and another teenager with long feet. The shoes were expensive. One day my grandmother came for a visit and found me in my bedroom, sitting on the side of the bed putting on socks. She sat beside me, took one of my feet in her hands, and, as she cradled it, commented that it was a fine foot, and that only royalty have a long, slender foot like that. The comment was said with such care and honest love and appreciation that I didn't stop to realize that she knew nothing about royalty. Her comments seemed reasonable to me and just made me feel good. She had selected her comments from a wide range of possibilities, which surely included the fact that those long feet were costing my parents money and that it would have been better if they were not so big.

My daddy often took my feet in his hands and said that it was wonderful how people are created in just the right dimensions. I was tall and wasn't it lucky that my feet were long so I could stand well, for if my feet were smaller, the fulcrum would be different; and he showed me how I would fall over easily. That would not only look awkward, but would feel awkward, too. How very wonderful for me that my feet were the size they were.

I came out of childhood thinking my feet were grand and that I was very lucky for their size. The soft, positive comments that I received in childhood influenced my thoughts about my feet. Had the comments been less than positive, my thoughts would likely be different.

Beginning very early in their lives, when either Lara or Julie sat on my lap, I gently rubbed the full length of her spine. I commented on the beauty and strength of the young back. I spoke of the wonder and sturdiness of the beautiful back and how it helped her to stand so straight. I often said it during quite musing times and usually with a quiet awe and appreciation. The girls heard the comments frequently from me during their forming years. All their lives, Lara and Julie have stood straight and tall, even to the point of our hearing from friends about the fine carriage they each have. Perhaps, it was an example of the twig growing in the direction in which it was encouraged.

Through the richness of my observations, and the richness of the focused stories of my childhood, I realized the long-lasting power of comments. Through Lara and Julie's childhood, Michael and I were keenly aware of our power to hurt and scar with words. We elected not to go down that path.

6 *I created a way to let my daughters get my attention.*

There were many situations when I was talking with an adult and my daughter wanted my attention in a non-emergency fashion. I thought it would be inappropriate to allow her to interrupt and become the center of attention simply because she wanted it. That would not be showing respect to the adult. I did not want her noticeably interrupting my conversation, but, at the same time, I wanted to show her that I knew she was important, too. I wanted to show her respect and also design a way that would let her learn respect for my guest and me.

I wanted her interruption and my response to be fluid. I knew that if I taught her to verbally interrupt, however kindly and properly, the attention would immediately transfer to us; and, depending upon the nature of the talking in progress, perhaps that kind of interruption would not be ideal. There are certain points at which her interruption would be easier and more smoothly accommodated. Lara had no way of knowing the proper timing, but I would know. We needed a signal. We decided upon a light hand squeeze.

When I saw Lara approaching me, I made sure that my hand that was closest to her was free of holdings. Lara would come and slip her hand in mine, an action usually undetected by the other person. If noticed, it appeared charming. I acknowledged her presence by a small squeeze but did not look at her. Instead, I continued looking at my guest as we talked. With the slight squeeze, I was saying to Lara, "I'll look for the very first spot to interrupt my conversation and turn to you." If it took a few minutes, I'd squeeze her hand again to let her know I had not forgotten her. All this time her hand remained in mine while she waited patiently.

It was important that we both upheld the agreement. She was to slip her hand in mine and wait patiently, trusting me to follow through as quickly as I could. I was to honor that trust by using my judgment to seek the interruptible moment and act on it as quickly as I reasonably could.

This process was in place from about ages two through six. After that, it was no longer needed; she had acquired a strong sense of good timing and a respectful way to interrupt on her own.

7 *Knowing what one's face presents is valuable information.*

When Julie was in morning kindergarten in Maryland, I used to collect her at noon each day. All the children ran out to meet their parent or their ride, waving papers and jumping around. Julie was very solemn faced as she came out and found me. She was not frowning or looking unhappy, she was more blank-faced. One day I asked her if she was happy to see me when she came out of the school door. She replied, "Oh, yes!" I told her that I couldn't tell for there was no look of recognition or pleasure on her face. Julie was dumbfounded; she had no idea that her face was not showing the pleasure she was feeling. She also expressed sadness that I had not known. I told her that until she was close enough for me to hear her words, I had only her face to guide me. From that time forward, Julie always looked easily and sincerely happy to see me. It showed on her face. I struggle to think what would have happened had I just assumed that that was the way Julie was and let her be. Had I not asked her, I would have given tacit approval to something Julie was not even aware of, and was not in her nature.

During this same time, Julie had a developing face that looked like a sad clown when she cried. The corners of her mouth went down and it made her face very funny looking. It was hard not to laugh when one saw her face. You can imagine that it was hard for me to comfort her when I saw that face. Knowing that a laughing mother and a hurt child did not properly match, I needed to help Julie and myself. One day when she cried, I told her what her face looked like and got a mirror for her to see. She slowly laughed when she saw her face. I told her how hard it was for me sometimes to care for her properly when I saw that face. There was very little she could do with her face at that time, but she was aware of what she was presenting. As her face developed, the funny-face-while-crying disappeared.

I tell my students that everyone should know what their faces look like when they are sad, angry, puzzled, happy, confused, interested, and frightened. Know what their faces look like when they cry, laugh, sob, and giggle. Studying one's face in a mirror as one tries on the faces helps one to see what is presented to the public. Using a mirror, close your eyes, feel happy, and allow happiness to show on your face. Then quickly open your eyes and consider if you saw your face right now would you think it was happy? Then try other emotions. If you don't like what you see in the mirror, you can make adjustments. If your happy face doesn't tell others that you are happy, you run a chance of being misread. If you think you are showing anger but your face doesn't reflect anger, you may be misleading those who are interacting with you.

8 *I made an agreement with each child to maintain a united front in public.*

I often saw children and parents interact with each other with ridicule or put-downs. What I saw seemed disrespectful to each. I saw children roll their eyes and say, "Oh, Mother," in a disparaging tone. I saw and heard parents make fun of their children in a disparaging way. I didn't want either path for my children and me. Instead, I wanted a way to establish respect between us.

I made an agreement with each child that she and I would never knowingly embarrass each other or other family members through words or tones or eye rolling when we were among other people. We discussed what we were not going to do. We agreed that we could trust each other; it would be a two-way street. We had to trust and be trustworthy, for either of us could misstep.

I never heard, "Oh, Mommy," said in a disparaging way and I feel confident that eyes were not rolled behind my back. Lara and Julie never heard me complain or fuss at them in front of their peers. The fussing and complaining from either of us was handled in private as a family matter.

One day, Julie called from school asking me if I could bring a paper to her. The paper was due that day and she had forgotten it. The night before, I had strongly suggested to Julie

LIFE TEACHINGS

that she put her paper in her schoolbag so she wouldn't forget it the next morning. She was cross and said that she would remember. When she called, her voice was normal and so was mine. I knew the set-up at school—that she was using a phone on a secretary's desk, and that the secretary was probably listening. Julie and I both knew that the united front would be maintained. She asked if I would be able to bring it to her. I said, yes, I could have it there within the hour. She thanked me and that was the end.

As Julie made the request of me, I quickly thought of how I would handle the situation if it were an adult, say, Michael at his work or a family friend. I would not berate either of them at their work, in front of people. I would not do that to Julie at her work. Julie and I both trusted that our respect would be in place. She and I also knew that if the situation were reversed, she would display respect for me. We both counted on it.

When Julie returned home that afternoon, we talked about the situation. She knew that she should have remembered the paper and she was sorry. She thanked me for bringing it to her. Together, we formed a plan that could prevent the same situation from occurring again. The plan gave Julie more responsibility and control over her life, while it respected the fact that I might not be available another time to deliver her paper. Julie had also seen the united front in action, and knew it could be initiated again if needed.

9 *Whenever I had information that I thought my daughters could use, I gave it to them.*

I particularly used this theory when we were going someplace new. I told them what I knew about the situation so they could be free to put their attention on other parts of the experience.

If we were going to the doctor, I described how the surroundings looked and how we could function successfully in the surroundings, if I knew. I told them why things were like they were. Going to a picnic, I'd describe the environment, who would be there, the food, if I knew-anything that I thought could help them feel confident in the upcoming situation. After all, I knew things that could help me interact and I wanted them to have the same useful information. That seemed fair to me. The talking was done as we traveled to the event so they had a few moments to absorb the information and make it useful. The girls became used to functioning with information that prepared them for an event or activity.

Once, after a quick exam, a doctor decided that Lara needed a shot. The decision was a total surprise to me and to her. Things moved quickly. Immediately a nurse appeared and began reaching for Lara's arm to give the shot. Lara squirmed in her seat and looked at me in bewilderment which made the nurse call for reinforcement as she anticipated balkiness. Then Lara really started fighting and the nurses were equally strong in trying to pin her down. I called a halt and asked them to wait a second; Lara just needed information. The nurses released their grips and I knelt to talk quickly and quietly to Lara. I explained that it needed to be done, she would be fine, and that this was not a choosing place for her. Things went more smoothly and the shot was administered without fuss on Lara's part.

Visiting relatives, going camping, shopping, and going to the laundromat-everything was available for talking to prepare. It was like painting a quick, fairly detailed picture for them. I wanted the girls to know at least the rudiments that I knew. They also saw the same behavior between Michael and me if we were heading into a new situation and one of us had information that the other did not. It seemed a fine way to share information and to prepare us for an experience.

To this day, we perform part of this procedure as we brief each other on the people we will see and their relationship to the event. Pooling information with interested parties, in a timely fashion, seems respectful.

10 *I called it "turning the viewpoint."*

Empathy was a word that the girls learned early in their lives. I started using the word and talking the concept with them as early as when Lara was two years old. I called it "turning the viewpoint." We played games imagining that we were in the body or head of a cow we were watching in the field. What do we see? How does the world look from his point of view? Does he have any concerns? Using this framework, we looked at the family dog, newspaper articles about people, victims of fire, and contest winners. It was easy when we had no vested interest in the person or animal. It was only an exercise at this point. We each added insight from what we were picturing or imaging as we turned our viewpoint to theirs. This was not done in a school-like fashion, but rather in an easy musing fashion.

Soon, we turned our attention to people and events we encountered, not just those we read about. If a seller at the farmer's market seemed cross, we played with possibilities that could explain her rudeness. If a sign told us to rinse our bodies before entering the swimming pool, we talked of why the owner felt a need for such a posting. If a classmate got into trouble for stamping her feet on her way to the pencil sharpener, we talked of what might have produced such behavior and what might be the teacher's reaction.

Through our exercises, it was clear that changing the viewpoint revealed many possibilities to us. Whether or not any of our thoughts were accurate did not change the fact that our exercises showed us that rarely was a behavior directed personally at us. Instead, the behavior was likely driven by aspects of the person's life that we didn't know. Turning the viewpoint taught us to take the spotlight off of ourselves and focus it more on another or an event. It further encouraged us to understand that we might react the same way if we were in the other person's shoes.

When we moved into sibling disputes, we moved into a vested arena. Here, we didn't always examine the other viewpoint for I didn't want it to be tedious for them and perhaps become a perfunctory activity. We mainly used "turning the viewpoint" when we were seeking to understand a possible reason behind some behavior or response. I felt that it was important for them to know that to understand the reason behind an action did not always mean that one agreed with the action. Understanding and agreeing could be two separate things.

By learning to change our viewpoint, we all bought the gift of time concerning a perplexing or hurtful person or situation, and often the benefit of the doubt. With this temporary benefit of the doubt, we often found out that things were not always as bad as they had initially seemed.

11 Geodes became our family's symbol of "more than meets the eye."

By understanding and practicing empathy, our family quickly realized that there usually was more to learn about people and situations. Probably there is more to something or someone than meets the eye.

Geodes, wonderful stones from the geological realm, became our family's symbol of "more than meets the eye." Geodes are rocks that are sphere-shaped and quite ordinary looking. They are grayish and have bumps on them. They are not the kind of rocks that garner attention; they blend in with the soil and other nondescript rocks. Geodes can be broken into, but it takes great effort with a saw and plenty of work and time. When geodes are halved, inside are remarkably beautiful worlds that are quite unlike the outer surface. Inside can be sparkles and colors, and sometimes ages-old water. It is an unexpected world of colored crystals and minerals arranged in beautiful patterns. No two geodes are exactly alike; the colors, the degree of sparkle, and the size vary greatly and grandly. The inside beauty cannot be detected from the outside, and the beauty is revealed only after effort.

As a family we took this to mean that what people show us probably is not all there is to them. Details of the richness and beauty inside people are not always readily apparent from the outside. If we want to know more, we will have to put forth effort. The insides of geodes differ because of the surrounding conditions and materials that were present during their forming. People differ because of the experiences in which they participate. To get to the fascinating part, we have to show interest, ask questions, and listen.

Oil and gemstones are not found on the earth's surface, and geodes do not break open without effort. Each is discovered by solid attention from the searcher. They do not volunteer themselves.

We began buying halves of geodes and placing them throughout the house to remind us that things and people are not always what they look like or seem. There is more than meets the eye. Like a geode, a person may be quite nondescript looking from the outside, but with attention from us in the form of questions, we may discover unexpected beauty.

Today, each member of our family, in our different homes and apartments, has geodes that remind us of what we know to be true. Things and people are more than what they seem— a concept that helps us avoid too quickly labeling or categorizing people and situations.

12 *Events and situations are framed through a lens.*

I wanted a solid way to help the girls understand how serious is the fact that there is more to most anything than what meets the eye. When the girls were four and five years old, I used a kite flying lesson to introduce this message. During our outing, we had a picnic, the girls searched for four-leaf clovers, we rode our bikes, we flew the kites, and we fed the ducks. We took pictures of most of the activities, and several views of some of them. Some pictures had both Julie and Lara in them, some had just one of the girls, and some had Michael and me in them, too.

Several days later, when we got the prints developed, we enjoyed reliving the fine outing. Our assignment was to pick only one picture to put in a scrapbook to represent the whole experience. Some pictures were not clear, the angle was not good, or someone's eyes were closed. After much discussion, we sadly narrowed the good pictures down to the required one and labeled it "kite-flying." "But, Mommy, we did so much more that day!" That one photograph said very little about the other events of the day. Indeed, the selected shot of the girls feeding the ducks did not show Julie getting bitten by the razor-sharp "teeth" of the same duck that looked so serene in the photograph. The biting happened just after the shot.

We realized that if any of us were to choose one photo by

ourselves, the selection would be different. There was a great one of Michael looking like a fine ballet star as he reached to get a kite that was entangled in a tree. Julie liked the one of the girls bending over looking for clovers, but Lara said that we couldn't see their faces. Lara liked the one at the picnic that showed ants running over the ice cream. The selected photograph would be one person's idea of what represented the whole situation. Other people may or may not agree.

Several months later Michael and I attended a high school football game. The girls were asleep when we came home so they heard nothing about the game until the next morning. As I started telling the girls about the game, I noticed a photograph in the morning newspaper of a fight that had occurred down by one of the goal posts after the game ended. That photograph is what readers of the newspaper saw of the game. I used that picture to reinforce our talk about there being more to the story.

I had seen the fight but I thought it was minor. What really intrigued me was when a small dog got loose from his owner and raced across the field to play with Johnny. Johnny was one of the dog's owners. Johnny was also one of the tackles for the home team. The dog's appearance created quite a stir as the game stopped while Johnny scooped up the dog and took him back to the stands. Exciting as it was to me, a photograph of the dog and Johnny was not in the morning's newspaper.

During the next months, we extended our understanding of this important concept to sad stories or rumors that we would hear about someone. We discussed how someone was selecting what we were being told just like someone selected the one photograph. We realized that there is likely more to a story, rumor, or situation than what we know. Upon hearing a story, if our first interpretation was negative or disbelief, we considered that we likely didn't have all of the information.

I felt that being slower to pass negative judgment was a fine attribute and would be useful in many situations in which Lara and Julie would later find themselves. However, I was quick to point out that, if at any time they perceived themselves in physical danger, it didn't matter whether or not there is more to the situation. Just get out of there. They could do their pondering of "more to the situation than meets the eye" from a safer distance.

13 *I felt that play was my daughters' work and it was very important.*

Play was highly valued in our home. I wanted our home to reflect that value.

During the first eight years of the girls' lives, we lived in several different states. We usually rented houses that had three bedrooms. In order to value the play, the very largest bedroom, a master bedroom with private bath, always became the playroom. The girls shared a room and Michael and I took the remaining room. We only slept in the smaller rooms during the evening, while the large playroom was used all day and sometimes into the early night. We thought that this was a better use of space and an easy way to reflect a value.

The children's play was not restricted to the playroom, but most often, they chose that space. They were never banished to the playroom for punishment.

Hung the length of the playroom was a clothesline. It was eye-level for the girls so they could hang their pictures themselves and easily see and appreciate their work. Nearly every day, there were fresh paintings and writings, hung with snap clothespins. Blue ribbons and other awards were also displayed here.

We did have a refrigerator door concept, but it was the clothesline in the playroom. Many families we knew used magnets to secure their children's special papers and drawings to the refrigerator. Every time a family member or guest went by the refrigerator or opened it, the works were visible and ready to be admired. Photographs, "A" or "star" papers, telephone numbers, and bills were also displayed. I don't remember any of Lara and Julie's early work being put on the refrigerator, for they had their lovely clothesline in the playroom. However, vowels or numbers that I was teaching them did go onto the refrigerator door. Years later, Lara occasionally sent me a sheet of data from her immunology research, and Julie occasionally sends a graph from a physical oceanography project of hers. Each paper is labeled "for the refrigerator." I still don't put them on the refrigerator, but the idea held.

The idea of putting artworks and important papers in a prominent place, and at eye level, showed in an odd way one summer day in Maryland. Lara and Julie had concocted a pet show for the neighborhood. It was a very loosely organized affair and the main emphasis seemed to be that every pet would receive an award. There were categories for every-thing—best one-eyed dog; best gray dog with white spots; best side-ways walking dog. You see the range of possibilities. The affair was over fairly quickly and the pet owners seemed inordinately pleased with the awards. Our little dog, Shelley, won an award, and later that day I saw it hung on the wall just above his dog dish—about five inches from the floor, just above the baseboard. They wanted Shelley to be reminded regularly how splendid he was, and since it was for him, it should be where he could see it. From their clothesline experience in the playroom, the girls had understood the value of knowing who composes an audience and then catering and adjusting to that audience.

Currently, we have a dog that goes into a cage in the kitchen when we are gone. Hung on the side of the cage for him to enjoy are three postcards of colorful animals - a parrot, two deer, and two dogs standing upright with fanciful hats on their heads. It is his own private art gallery, at his eye level.

In the playroom, all toys, books and play items were kept on child-height shelves, not scattered in a toy box. In this way, all pieces were kept together ready for the next play. The integrity of the item was maintained. I did not know how orderly the girls would choose to be in their later years, but I did want them to know how to be orderly. For the eight years we had a playroom, the influence of orderliness was present. We all liked how the tidy playroom looked at the beginning of a day. The orderliness seemed to invite play, for the items were lined up and ready. Of course, if, at the end of the day, play was in progress, those items were kept out.

In the playroom were tools for the children's work. There was always a small-sized table and chairs, crayons, many sizes of plain paper, markers, tape, paste, and wood pieces to fashion what the mind was thinking. Mainly, we favored wooden toys over plastic ones so the little hands would feel a natural quality. In the playroom were other things like a small record player, wooden blocks, a cradle that grandfather built, dolls, stickers, dress-up items and books, always books. Many of the things in the playroom came from garage sales.

Whenever the pick-up and put-away activity became weary for the girls because so many things were on the floor, Michael and I helped. We each picked up and put away five single items. The size of the item didn't influence the count. After we each picked up five items, we surveyed the results. The results were always quite grand for we had five items times four people. Then the project seemed doable and we all worked to put the remaining crayons or blocks into their containers and onto a shelf. If the room was extra messy, we each picked up another five items which now made forty pieces. That surely made a noticeable difference.

No privileges were ever withheld if the playroom was not cleaned up; instead, we all just helped. Sometimes, a messy playroom delayed a departure for a very brief time. It was minor.

My daddy had used the idea of the five-item pick-up and put-away and I remembered that it had made sense to me when I was a child. Five items was such a small number and it required very little effort; but look at the result if everyone picked up five at the same time. Of course, this activity was also showing the power and quick results of cooperative behavior.

14 *I valued the imagination and relevance that books could bring to a life.*

During the very earliest years, I bought beautiful award-winning picture books and classic picture books. When money was tight, I cut back on other things in order to buy a picture book each month. I elected to buy rather than to go to the library at this stage. I wanted the girls to be surrounded by permanent books that were theirs. From the beginning, they were shown how to handle books with respect and to put them away on the small shelves.

The beauty of the pictures and the thoughtful text were highly attractive to all of us. Michael or I often read the books to the girls, and we noticed that they loved to "read" the books themselves. The stories that they would tell or "read" to the dog, to each other, or to a doll were very elaborate and sometimes more interesting than the actual text. I liked hearing their imagination at work as I listened to this crafted world of theirs.

Since I value books, it seems logical that I also would value the ability to read well. I soon found myself teaching the girls to read. I did not use any pre-packaged material; but I did use their ideas. I taught the girls to read the phonetic way. I drew pictures for the vowels and later wrote very small stories that had Lara or Julie as the star. The picture vowels were displayed at their eye level on the refrigerator door.

By the first grade, each daughter was reading chapter books. I bought loads of books at garage sales. For many years, the piece de resistance Christmas present was their own private box of about thirty garage sale books. The cost to Michael and me was very small, and the present was received as a special, grand one. The thirty books became sixty as they took places on the playroom's child-height bookshelves that Lara and Julie shared.

Through books, the girls learned concepts that they applied to life situations. They recognized Brer Rabbit's Briar Patch when they happened upon a particular situation, or indeed, when they themselves crafted a similar situation. They understood Achilles' Heel and the Trojan Horse and the powerful concepts portrayed. At the time, these concepts gave us all a common language. As they got older, they saw that many people had this same useful common language.

At least once in their early childhood, I remember information from a book helping to calm a troubling situation for the girls. During our first year in Minnesota, the girls came upon a pond in their exploration of the fields around the house. It was a hot day so they took off their sandals and began wading in the cool water. It wasn't very long before they came running down the dirt road, crying and hollering for help. They each had long, black leeches all over their bare legs. They had no idea what the leeches were, but they stung, and the situation felt frightening and desperate. As Michael and I struggled to release the leeches' hold on their legs, we commented that Laura Ingalls had found herself in a similar plight. This surprising bit of information calmed the girls for a moment or two as they took a closer look. The grimaces remained plentiful, however.

15 *The girls learned to recognize and reach for opportunities in creative ways.*

We lived in California when the girls were ages two-and-a-half and four. I was interested in a Montessori pre-school for both daughters since I was quite impressed with the Montessori philosophy encouraging self-reliance and independence. I got to know the local teacher quite well and realized that she would be a dynamite teacher for the girls.

Michael and I were able to afford five mornings a week for Lara. We could not afford to send Julie that often and, she was, after all, eighteen months younger. We were able to pay for two mornings a week for her.

The teacher knew of our strong interest in the Montessori style of learning and suggested something wonderful. She said that sometimes a child misses class because of illness or conflicts in family calendars. She proposed that Julie be dressed and ready to attend Montessori each day that we brought Lara. If there were a vacancy, Julie would take the spot. The teacher's kind reasoning was that the position was already paid for and Julie could take the vacancy without additional charge.

I was enormously touched by the teacher's thoughtfulness and generosity. Julie, at age two, understood the process, and was dressed and ready to attend each morning when we checked Lara in. On average, Julie was able to attend two extra mornings a week that year. If there was not a vacancy, Julie returned home, played in the playroom or helped me with errands and chores until it was time to collect Lara at Montessori. Interestingly, Julie didn't cry or show frustration if there was not a vacancy. She understood the agreement and knew that only through that arrangement could she possibly attend more than two classes a week. Within our family, we spoke often of the teacher's remarkable kindness to us.

Years later, this method to obtain additional learning showed up again in Julie's life, only this time it was at her own initiative. During the summer after her fifth grade, she decided she wanted to study a foreign language like Lara. Lara was alternating language classes each day and studying various levels of Spanish, German, and French. Julie's elementary school started each day at 9:15. She knew that the local Junior High began at 8:00. Julie contacted the first level Spanish teacher, asking if she could sit in on the first Spanish Level I section of the morning and leave at the conclusion of class each day to go to the beginning class at her elementary school. Julie was delighted when the teacher agreed. I think the teacher was surprised at the odd request as she honored a learner's proposal.

In high school, Lara and Julie each took five levels of all three languages offered (German, French, Spanish). They went every other day to one or the others. When Lara first proposed this arrangement to her teachers, she stated that she would quickly notify them if the arrangement was not working. Further, it was understood that she would be responsible for all classroom assignments and would not receive extra attention. The request was a first for the high school and the teachers were very gracious to Lara. The format was in place when Julie came along and made her request. In addition to the three languages, Julie also picked up Chinese that was suddenly offered for a semester by a visiting teacher from China.

Both girls did very well with the languages and enjoyed themselves. The only time it got a bit tricky for them was at final exam time. Sometimes the testing schedule required them to take one language test right after another. A needed verb, but in German, might appear in their minds while they were taking a Spanish test. Neither daughter seemed to spend an unusual amount of studying time with the increased course load. They were skillful at recognizing patterns, and the additional language studies seemed to be easy for them.

Years earlier, the remarkable Montessori teacher had proposed a way for Julie to get additional experiences. Lara and Julie recognized the proposal as a fine opportunity to take advantage of education that was already in place and ready to be accessed in a positive way. Later they used their understanding of this concept to craft further experiences for themselves with foreign language courses. Now that they are adults, they continue to use this understanding to recognize and reach for experiences that are available to them.

16 *I felt that it was important for my daughters to understand the remarkably strong role that preparation plays in determining the quality of experiences.*

I wanted them to see that preparation was normal and easily apparent in many places in their lives already.

We began by noticing that we prepared to cook by buying groceries; we put covers on our beds to prepare for sleep; we cleaned our house to prepare for guests, and we packed things in our red Volkswagen camper to prepare for travel. We filled the tub with water and had a towel nearby as we prepared for a bath; and we straightened the playroom at night to prepare for the next day's play. If preparation was not done for any of these activities, we still had the event; but the girls noticed that things went a little more smoothly in these simple, daily activities if we prepared.

I also wanted Lara and Julie to see that they didn't need preparation in order to exist or to enter into experiences. I did not want them to feel guilty or restricted if they hadn't prepared. However, I did want them to see that preparation could make a positive difference in how they lived, in what happened to them, and in the degree to which they interacted with their world.

Sometimes procrastination tries to crowd out preparation. Then one has a choice-procrastination or preparation.

Sometimes, it is highly appropriate to procrastinate. After all, the dog probably doesn't really need to be washed today; those bed sheets don't really have to be washed today; and certainly, the dirty dishes can wait until a later time. Sometimes though, it is better to get on with it, to prepare and not procrastinate. The cold Minnesota winters will be easier if we prepare by getting our fuel oil tank filled before November; by seeing that our car battery is sound; and by seeing that our winter boots are leak proof, have warm linings and fit. The winter is easier if we arrange to have enough bales of alfalfa delivered for the pony before the snow arrives.

As the girls got older, our talking emphasized other things. An employment interviewer will be more impressed with us if we know something about the interviewer's company. Test scores will be higher if we study the material. I felt that the concept of preparation was so very important for the girls to grasp. Frequently, choosing timely preparation would give them more resources with which to interact with their environment. Again, interaction that would help form them.

If there is a question about where to begin preparation or what form the preparation should take, a quick survey can set things moving. Ask, "In order to get the most out of this situation, what do I need to know or do before I enter this arena?"

I thought that understanding preparation as a normal aspect of life was a sound one. Years later, one of my very bright students encountered a situation where her preparation was rewarded. Sarah entered a West Coast university as a first-year student interested in a biology major. Because of her prior success in a high school mentorship with a University of Minnesota researcher, she was interested in aligning herself with a well-known biologist at her new school. The professor had a solid reputation for not wanting contact with first- or second-year students. Sarah knew this but called and requested a meeting anyway, acknowledging that she was a first-year student and requested a meeting with him. He very begrudgingly agreed to give her just ten minutes of his time.

Once she secured the appointment, Sarah went to the campus library and found journal articles that detailed the research in which the professor and his lab members were involved. She studied all of the articles until she understood them well.

When her meeting came, Sarah talked to the professor about his work, asking questions and listening carefully to the answers. She carried her part of the conversation. After thirty minutes of the interaction, the professor asked Sarah what he could do for her. She replied that she wanted to work in his lab, and she wanted him to guide her studies for the next four years. She also wanted him to introduce her to people in the field and to point out opportunities to her in biology. The professor readily agreed and Sarah was to begin her research in his lab the following week.

The story, so far, is a good one about the fine role of preparation, but now the story turns. Sarah was elated and went back to her dorm to share her good news. Her peers were astonished and asked how she could have had such success since the professor did not interact with first-year students. When she told them of her preparation, one of her friends asked, "Isn't that cheating?"

No, preparation is not cheating. No, the advantage is not unfair. Expect to prepare. Actors prepare for their show by rehearsing lines and staging for many days. Athletes prepare for their game by practicing and training for many hours. Actors and athletes know that preparation is necessary for them to perform their jobs well. So it is with all of us.

17 *Not being able to afford something can be a luxury.*

It seemed reasonable to me that, as functioning members of a family, children should be told from the very youngest age when money is scarce. The question is how. There were many times during the girls' childhood when our family budget would not allow a particular toy or outing. From talking to other parents and reading how-to books, I knew that some parents elected to tell children when money was low and others elected not to tell. It seemed reasonable to me that children should be told from the very youngest age when money is scarce. It would surely be a situation in which they would find themselves many times during their independent lives. So, to tell was the first decision. Then came the how.

I could readily see that the manner and attitude with which the no-money information was transferred would be crucial. If I acted in tone, words, and manner that it was okay and not scary, things could more easily be kept in perspective. It would be an honest telling, for the financial circumstances in which we found ourselves at times were never scary, just lean.

Michael and I used the words, "No money right now," to Lara and Julie rather than, "can't afford it." If the topic were a toy, we four would muse together about how the girls would play with the toy if we had the money to buy it. We spent the time playing with the idea of the toy, and even deciding where we would put it in the playroom. After time spent musing like this, the toy seemed to get played out. When money became a little more available, rarely was that same toy the one they wanted to spend money on.

During the process, Michael and I did not feel guilty because we couldn't buy it. After all, there were many requests that had received a yes. The balance between yes and no was remembered by all of us.

This easy, matter-of-fact technique was one I remembered from my own childhood. It did not concern money, but it did concern something that was not going to happen.

During one extra hot Kentucky week, with no air-conditioning in our house, my siblings and I thought it would be a grand and helpful idea to fill our basement with water. Then all members of the family would have a place during the daytime where we could be cool. Daddy and Mama sprawled out on the grass with us one evening as we explained and cajoled. Daddy didn't get to the no right away; instead, in an easy musing voice, he asked us questions that set us to thinking how it would work. We were excited, for we felt that he was interested in our project.

Daddy mixed easy questions with hard ones. None of our solutions were nixed. We just kept talking about how nice it would be. After a while, we, by ourselves, thought of some problems with our idea. Daddy didn't have to say no. We sadly knew from our thinking and easy talking that our idea only worked on a superficial basis. Later, this way of allowing the children to sort things out seemed useful as a way to put matters into perspective when money was lean. And, it did turn out to be very useful. I readily saw that part of the pleasure of things is in the playing, not necessarily in the owning.

I again experienced this concept in the very early years of our marriage. Michael and I fancied white French Provincial bedroom furniture. We certainly couldn't afford the matching set we both wanted. However, we played with how it would look, where the pieces would be placed, and what would be kept in the drawers. None of this easy talking took much time, but over the years, I saw that we were finished with it. When we finally were able to buy our bedroom pieces, it was not white French Provincial, nor was it a matched set. We were through with that dream for we had finished our playing. We had received a bit of understanding that there could be luxury in not being able to afford something.

Most of our outings with the children were without cost. Parks, kite flying, gold panning, and pole fishing from a riverbank were favorites. We nearly always took our own food and called it a picnic since we were eating away from home. We often ate in the camper or at roadside tables or sitting on rocks alongside a stream. Buying fast food was rare for us. Zoos and museums often had a free day and sometimes there were fireworks and out-door symphonies and performances to enjoy. To us the pleasure was in the doing, not in the cost.

18 *I instinctively knew that I wanted my daughters to have their own fears, not mine.*

I was keenly aware that all humans have fears and I realized that this was an area that needed to be addressed. I instinctively knew that I wanted my daughters to have their own fears, not mine. Worse yet would be if they had their fears and mine. I wanted to avoid displaying my fears for the first ten years of their lives. I thought that by the time they were ten, my influence in that arena would be less.

I did avoid transferring most, if not all, of my fears to my daughters. I had, and still have, a fear of flying, a fear of heights, and a great uneasiness about snakes. I didn't know the basis of my fears, I just know I have them. None of the three were crippling or serious enough to keep me from family involvement, however.

We did not fly during those early years of their lives. We simply had no money for it. We drove everywhere in our bright red, second-hand VW camper. My fear of heights was tested every time we climbed to look over a ledge to see how far we had come or to see something pretty. I just didn't stand quite as close to the edge as the rest of the family. Michael and I had agreed to not talk about my fear of heights and I made sure that my body language did not reflect that fear. I did my share of talking about what we were seeing so everything seemed normal. One of the rougher times for me was when we took a sky-lift. I just didn't lean over too far to look at the interesting things that were directly under us. And, it was soon over. I realized that if we emphasized Mommy's fear of heights, I would receive the attention instead of the pretties in front of us, under us, and all around us. It would be a misuse of attention.

I figured that my uneasiness around snakes would never have a circumstance to present itself. I was wrong. When Lara was six years old and Julie was four, we moved to Minnesota and to a farmhouse with lots of land around us. The land had trees, bushes, prairie, and space. Within this remarkable playground, the girls had a childhood of curiosity, climbing, exploring, and ponies. Several times they caught a harmless snake or two and brought it to me to stroke and feel its skin. By my keeping the focus on the importance of the moment and not on my uneasiness, I touched and exclaimed. I didn't behave this way to be a martyr—I did it because it seemed best.

Earlier, when the girls were very young, we encountered a wayward snake. One day I was standing by the bathroom sink arranging my hair. Lara and Julie were riding their tricycles up and down the hallway. We were in the last stages of preparing to go grocery shopping. Suddenly, Lara with wonderment and curiosity in her voice, announced, "Mommy, there is a snake by your legs!" I knew it had to be true for who could make that up? In a normal voice, I said, "There is?" Then I took a step or two backwards to see for myself. We all bent down to see an eight-inch long snake halfway out of an opening in the baseboard. Sure enough, at the spot where my legs had been.

"Ah, the little one must have taken a wrong turn and is lost and probably quite scared to see us. There must be a small opening that attracted him. Let's call Daddy (who is a veterinarian). He'll know what to do with the snake."

We kept a close eye on the snake while we waited for Michael and saw our visitor retreat into the opening. By the time Michael arrived, the snake was gone. We plugged the opening with cloth so the snake would not get distracted again from his normal path.

We all laugh at the retelling of the story today. Lara continues her role telling me of odd animals that are around me. The other day we were at the grocery. As I reached to select the mustard, Lara leaned over to me and whispered in my ear, "Mommy, there is a great big rabbit right behind you!" I laughed knowing that there would indeed be a great big rabbit behind me when I turned around to see. I turned, and there was a person dressed as a rabbit, as tall as I am and nearly on top of me. She never comments on the animals until they are very close to me.

19 *There was a fear that I carried into motherhood that I couldn't bypass.*

I couldn't pretend it didn't exist. It was so much a part of my cell memories that I knew it would be present. I decided I must turn it into a positive lesson for us all.

My mother and her best friend were killed in a car accident during the winter of my junior year of college. The road was icy and Mama was driving the car. I received the news as my history final exam was being distributed. The suddenness of the event, and the loss of someone whom I admired and who had had an important influence on my life, felt exceedingly harsh, and left me bewildered.

My mother's death imprinted upon me a solid realization of the fragileness of life and of the reality that life can end without warning. This imprint resulted in at least two of my life-long behaviors. First, I developed a strong understanding that I was to experience and be mindful of people and situations around which I found myself, for I could not know how long they would be around me. I acquired a real *enjoy the moment* understanding of life that became easy for me to live. Secondly, I became acutely concerned for the safety of loved ones who are traveling. I keep my good thoughts for their safety until I know that they are finished with their trip. They call and tell me they have arrived and are safe.

It was a courtesy in our family to call home if we were delayed from an expected arrival time; and we explained the delay. There was no passing of judgment about the reasons for the delay. The emphasis was on the courtesy of notifying each other before uneasiness set in. As the girls began driving and becoming more independent, they did not deviate from this. Still today as they return to their own homes from a visit with Michael and me, they always call or leave us a message that they are home safely. If they are spending the night away from their own homes, they tell us where they will be and the telephone number where they can be reached. Then they call later to let us know they are back home. They see this reporting not as an invasion of their privacy, but as a proper courtesy. I do the same for them. I continue to be enormously pleased at my daughters' consistent thoughtfulness on this matter that is so very important to me. And, I tell them of my appreciation.

I think keeping me informed made logical sense to my daughters as courtesy and respect. Then it became a mutual safety for each of us. Their uneasiness about my whereabouts and safety were alleviated if I remembered the courtesy also. They each know now, of course, the tie-in to my mother's death, but the courtesy of the behavior makes sense on its own.

20 *There are times when situations just do not make good sense.*

At home, we could always discuss a situation and adjust a highly illogical procedure or outcome. But outside the home, there were times when logic couldn't adjust an illogical situation. I would explain to my daughter that she was in a totally illogical situation and, in order to exit sanely, she needed to go along with the event. Could she do it? Upon hearing that explanation, she always said yes and proceeded to get through the matter. Perhaps, it was just my validating that, indeed, yes, I also saw it as she did-a totally nonsensical situation.

Lara was seven years old when we moved to Minnesota from Maryland. She entered fourth grade and hit a rough spot in her math lessons of long division. Lara had been taught a slightly different way of showing her work. Her new teacher refused to count a problem correct if it were not processed in the way that she preferred. Lara was getting the correct answers and showing all the processes she was using, but she was, through habit, using the way she had been taught in Maryland. The teacher called Lara and me in for a conference and announced that Lara would not pass the long division aspect of math class if she did not conform. She agreed that Lara was getting correct answers—one of a very few students in the class who was, and she agreed that Lara was showing her work. She added, however, that there was a particular way that she wanted the work shown. Lara and I left the conference and walked home talking about the dilemma in which we found ourselves. Finally, I stopped, turned, and looked at her. I told her the situation was nuts. It was illogical but it also carried a high price tag. It needs to be done the way the teacher wants. Can you do it? What can we do to help you remember to do it that way? We came up with some ways to help her remember, and we moved on from there. Lara did pass long division.

Once when Lara was about ten years old, she spent the night at a friend's house where she ran into a perplexing situation. At breakfast the next morning, she was asked how many pieces of toast she wanted. She was told her friend wanted two. Lara had no idea but said that would be fine for her, too. She began eating the toast, got full, and didn't eat all of it. Her friend's mother told her that she had ordered it and that she could not leave the table until she finished. Both became stubborn. Soon the mother called, telling me the situation. I asked her to put Lara on the phone. From Lara's point of view, she had played it right. She had politely eaten and gotten full. It was over, she thought. Lara did not need to explain anything to me for I could see how it looked to her. On the phone, I told Lara that the situation was illogical, Lara was right, but the mother had the control. Would it be possible for Lara to eat the rest of the toast? It would make her friend's mother feel better, while Lara and I agreed on the non-logic of the situation.

Lara said yes, hung up the phone, sat down and ate the rest of the toast. The mother was pleased that this wayward child had decided to mind. And, Lara didn't need to retort because she knew that I agreed with her.

This is not a technique that I would overuse. And very rarely was it needed. But, there were times when it was enormously helpful to cement family concepts and beliefs. I knew that as she got older, Lara would find herself in non-life-threatening situations that made no sense and she would have to deliver in order to exit. I wanted her to be able to trust her own reading of a situation even if she decided she had to perform opposite her common sense.

21 *I looked for ways to honor logical reasoning.*

In my life, neither logic or emotion has the reins, but one most often leads the other. I value both logic and emotion. I use logic to form a foundation of facts; then my heart takes the logic and helps with interpretation and action. It seems reasonable that I would value logic since I was always seeking the why of people, situations, and events. Once I had the logic in place, I would question whether something made sense according to what I already knew. I also examined whether something seemed fair in light of what I already knew.

It seemed to me that if I used this same approach in raising my daughters, they also would walk with both logic and emotion, and their emotions would rarely walk without logic. Early in their lives, Lara and Julie were encouraged consistently to view a situation with logic, and they were rewarded when the reasoning they expressed was sound. The reward was not treats or money; instead, the reward was that the situation went the way they had reasoned. In this way, I hoped to encourage wise decision-making. I looked for ways to honor the reasoning.

At first, the reasoning showed up in simple ways. Lara suggested that her long curly hair did not need washing tonight because it was not dirty. She had not been playing outside and her hair did not look or smell dirty. A minor thing, and her expressed logic made sense, so it was honored. "That's a good point, it makes sense, we won't wash it tonight." Julie tells me it is Lara's turn to wash the dishes. Lara says it is Julie's turn. "Remind me, I don't remember." Lara reminds us that she splashed dishwater on the floor and her clothes the night before as she plopped a skillet into an over-filled sink. Lara is right. Julie washes the dishes.

Sometimes, emotions led and logic followed. Julie wanted to wear a particularly favorite dress on a family outing. No reason, she just felt like wearing that particular plaid dress. The logic was expressed in a thoughtful manner. There was no reason not to wear it. She thought she would take a sweater so the outfit would be as warm as the one I wanted her to wear. The dress was worn.

As they got older, both girls noticed the value of logic in the family. When logic was used, the rewards were consistent. Lara and Julie realized that most anything could turn their way if the reasoning process was sound. There was no need to cajole me if the expressed logic showed thought and made sense. If the logic did not conflict with something major in the family, it was honored if at all possible. In this way, Lara and Julie were developing a way to use their minds and intuition. More and more, they trusted their own wisdom as Michael and I rewarded and encouraged their logical reasoning.

The mind was highly valued in my own childhood home by my parents, and expressed logical reasoning was honored. I had exited my own childhood and entered adulthood without knowing or living the concept of guilt. It never occurred to me that my childhood was fairly unique.

Lara and Julie also entered adulthood without the concept of guilt. That also seemed normal except that within the last several years, each of us knows more and more people who clearly have guilt as a functioning aspect of their lives. These adults acknowledge that the feeling of guilt concerning a particular event has no logic to it, but they still feel the emotion. Many of these same people have taken the concept even further and declare that another person creates the guilt they feel. They choose to think of the situation in this fashion rather than to see that it is their own choice of responses to the event that sets up the guilt rather than the other person making them feel guilty.

As I increasingly understand the concept of guilt, I suspect that consistent honoring of reason and logic from very early in the girls' lives left them free of guilt. Logic forced them to examine the ways of something, to understand the reasoning behind something. They could easily see if a decision was ruled only by emotion. Emotions were never thrown out, but we always wanted to know if logic was in the picture, too.

I hear that some parents seem able to keep control of children's behavior by warning that God will punish them if they do not do a particular something. If I had dared take such a tactic, the response from Lara and Julie would have been,

"How do you know that, Mommy?' Which meant, of course, what is that based on? Or, "I thought God loved me and was kind." Which meant, of course, "Where is the logic? I have thought this out; my logic makes sense, so God would understand that my action is fair. God would not be inconsistent."

Once when Lara was in the fourth grade in Minnesota, she was in the cafeteria buying her lunch. An older boy came up to her and said, "God wants you to give me your lunch." The boy obviously thought that the threat of God's displeasure was a productive statement; perhaps one that had worked when someone used it on him. Lara's reply was snappy and quickly delivered. "God prefers me to have my own lunch today," she stated as she walked to the table with her lunch firmly in hand.

Encouraging a child to pursue thinking and logical reasoning means that standards are high for all family members. No one in our family could make statements designed to control that were based on little reasoning. If I wanted a certain behavior from Lara and Julie, then it was my wanting it, not God or someone else. And, I had to know and express my reasoning. Sometimes though, an "I don't know, I just want this. Can we?" was good enough coming from Michael, me, Lara, or Julie. Sometimes the heart has to be honored without its usual companion of logic.

Recently, Lara told me about one of her supervisors who drove into the office on a Saturday morning to get a report that he was hoping Lara had completed. The completed work was not on her desk. When he told Lara on Monday of his long drive to the office and not finding the report, he waited for her explanation and statement of regret. Instead, she replied, "You mean you chose to come in on a Saturday to get a report when you knew that I would notify you when it was ready?" He laughed and said, "You really don't play with guilt, do you?"

To say that we as a family did not value guilt does not mean that we did not value responsibility. When we made a mistake, we had no guilt, but we had the responsibility to learn from the event and not repeat the mistake, or certainly not in the same way.

Like all children, Lara and Julie had many opportunities to make decisions away from home. And, like all people, sometimes these decisions did not look too good in hindsight. At the time of the decision, the girls were expected to use all their information and logic. The decision would be good based on the moment. That judgment was trusted. It was understood that Lara or Julie, who were in the moment, had more information than Michael or I. They were there and we were not, so of course, their judgment had to be honored. Later, if hindsight brought more information and showed that the decision should have been different, it still remained clear that with the information on hand at the time, the decision was logical. It made sense. Hindsight information was useful for the next experience.

22 *Michael's hearing liability resulted in an asset for the girls.*

Michael became hard of hearing as a two-year-old child. He didn't buy hearing aids until he was in his mid 50s, so the girls were raised with a father who was nearly deaf in one ear and had poor hearing in the other. For most of his life, Michael read lips.

As the girls began to talk in sentences, they were instructed to speak clearly and fairly loudly. There was no need to shout, but they were not to speak too softly. The request was a logical one so Michael could be involved. Initially, the girls were not told why, for speaking clearly and fairly loudly seemed to us to be a good life skill. The girls were also expected to look at us as they talked and keep their faces unblocked. They were not to have their hands in front of their mouths. They were told that many people look at the mouth as well as hear the words, so in order to best be understood, the girls needed to provide both a clearly visible face and clear words. We told them that Daddy hears better if he can see people's mouths, and that there are many others in the world who are like Daddy. We also told them that if they did not block their faces, and if they spoke clearly and distinctly, they could speak naturally and would have no need to speak either haltingly or with undue emphasis.

As a natural result, both Lara and Julie emerged from

childhood looking people in the eye as they spoke distinctly, straightforwardly, and a bit louder than many young people.

There are certainly times when the voice needs to be soft; particularly when one is talking about sadness, or explaining a hurt. At these times, the girls were naturally on our laps, or sitting beside us, as they were being comforted. The attention was so focused during these moments that Michael had little trouble hearing them.

One day when Lara and Julie were both still less than ten years old, one of my sisters remarked that the girls spoke loudly. My sister had a child of her own and also taught second grade students. She noticed a difference between how Lara and Julie spoke compared to others. She said that Lara and Julie were not overly loud, but certainly not soft. My sister's comments made me realize this for the first time. I reminded her of Michael's hearing; and said that I had forgotten how we had emphasized looking at people, showing the face, and speaking out loud. That night as I thought further, I realized that the girls had developed fine beginning communication skills because of their Daddy's hearing loss.

Today, both Lara and Julie display confidence as they communicate with others. They look people in the eye, while presenting a face without barriers, and speak distinctly in natural tones and rhythms. Michael's hearing liability ended up being an asset for the girls.

23 *We sought to add imagination and fancifulness to regular family activities.*

To Michael and me, imagination seems to be a very powerful aspect of creativity and playfulness. We wanted the girls to recognize and know how to create playfulness and fancifulness as a natural part of their lives.

For about six years, Michael told the girls stories about an ordinary looking caterpillar which turned into a beautiful butterfly that could go anywhere in the world. The girls loved the butterfly stories and regularly asked for them. Michael had a genius for making up the stories. They were clever, fanciful and had fascinating cultural or issue aspects to them. These were usually bedtime stories, were quite long, and were never repeats. The stories were magical, intelligent, and charming. The girls never tired of them and now that they are in their late twenties, the butterfly stories are mentioned fondly. The memory has wonderfully survived time's analytical look.

Before she could read, Lara told wonderful magical stories to Julie as they looked at picture books. Julie thought Lara was reading a story to her and was quite taken with Lara's ability. I often saw them sitting very close together at one end of the sofa, Julie with favorite blanket in hand and pacifier in mouth, being enchanted as Lara, with great confidence and flair, read to Julie from a book Julie had selected.

Julie, in turn, "read" wonderful magical stories to her dolls and stuffed animals that she positioned around her in the playroom. Her stories were so fanciful that I remember thinking that Julie would be disappointed when she was able to really read what was on the page. Her stories were so grand and exciting-the actual words in the books were quite mundane.

By regularly reading out loud, both girls developed a strong imagination and they also developed very strong reading-out-loud voices. They read with emphasis, exciting rhythm, and a variety of tones, for after all, each was entertaining-Lara was performing for Julie and Julie was performing for her dolls and stuffed animals.

Julie also took our cat, Kitty, for long rides through the house in a vehicle she had fashioned by taking a large box top and attaching a string that she could use to pull the box. Julie dressed Kitty in a baby sweater and a matching hat and placed her in the box. She dragged the box and Kitty all over the house, keeping up a lovely commentary of the sights that Kitty was seeing. Kitty and Julie never tired of the entertainment; and Lara and I were charmed by the sight of the two and by Julie's imaginative descriptions.

As in most families, Lara and Julie made many of the presents they gave to each other and to Michael and me. In addition to the handmade presents and drawings, the birthday chair was always festooned with long one-inch colorful cotton ribbons. They were tied and draped around the chair in a hap-hazard fashion, but the chair always seemed special.

Those same ribbons festooned the ponies on many occasions. For several years, Lara and Julie organized a family Fourth of July parade. Only Lara and Julie and our animals were in the parade, and only Michael and I were around to watch, but a parade we had. Daisy, the youngest Shetland, wonderfully festooned with ribbons, had Lara on her back holding a festooned Shelly dog, the family poodle. Julie followed, sitting on Gypsy, the older Shetland. Gypsy was equally festooned, and Julie held the beautifully festooned, and fussy, Kitty. The parade moved slowly past Michael's and my lawn chairs; and kept parading back and forth while Michael and I applauded and shouted positive comments. It was quite an affair as you can see.

Up through the middle school years, for each of the girls' birthdays, Michael, birthday hat on head, rode festooned Gypsy, and led festooned Daisy up the dirt road to meet the school bus. It was always a fun sight for the girls to find Michael and the two ponies waiting for them. Their bus mates were quite taken with the whole matter. Today, the girls say there was some embarrassment, but delight far overruled. When they alighted from the bus, Michael would get off Gypsy and the girls would get on the ponies; and thus they would come home to begin the celebration.

Many years later, when Lara married, Daisy was the guest of honor at the outdoor ceremony. Daisy was just off to the side, watching her friend and playmate get married. The event took place in the same backyard where Daisy had played with Lara and Julie for many years. Now, Daisy was again festooned, but this time with a beautiful custom-made garland of flowers woven through her mane and tail. When the florist first heard who this honored guest would be, there was a beat or two of silence before he quickly took a can-do attitude. At first, he thought of a hat. Lara and Julie were horrified. Lara quickly explained that Daisy was not a circus performer, but was indeed a special guest. Then the attention turned to getting measurements of the length of Daisy's mane and tail and selecting the colorful flowers.

Today, both Lara and Julie have an entertaining way about them; and imagination shows in their activities, in word play, and in descriptions. There is much laughter and playfulness about each of them. Imagination is an aspect of their approach to life.

24 *I thought that all similar-age children would be good playmates for my girls.*

That seemed very democratic to me and very proper. Between Lara's second and fifth years, we lived in Davis while Michael was getting further schooling at the University of California. Davis was wonderfully diverse in cultures and nationalities, and I was delighted that Lara and Julie would be involved in worlds that were different from theirs. I also wanted their ears exposed to accents other than my southern one and their voices to have less of a southern touch. In our immediate neighborhood lived several young international children. Lara and Julie enjoyed playing with the children and were richer for the experience.

At a certain point, a new boy joined the neighborhood who was a few years older than the rest. It soon became clear that he was interrupting play by pushing, calling names, and talking in ways that I didn't want for Lara and Julie. In addition, the neighborhood children were afraid of the new boy. A mother talked with his parents, but nothing changed.

This was a difficult time for me, for I had thought it important that Lara and Julie play with all children. I soon realized that this boy would influence the girls in ways that were quite contrary to how they were being raised. I knew that I was not going to turn my girls over to a child who was just forming himself and that, indeed, I needed to say no to the influence. I talked to Lara and Julie and told them my thoughts. I spoke of the importance and responsibility a parent has to form a child. There was no disagreement from them; instead, there was relief, for playing with the boy was stressful for Lara and Julie. Before we got very far into our plans of how to avoid the boy, his family moved from the neighborhood.

When I talked with Lara and Julie, I discovered that they welcomed a reason or excuse not to play with the unruly boy. I would not have known their feelings if we had not discussed the matter. Lara and Julie had information that helped me more fully understand. As we exited this troubling situation, the girls realized that they could have control over which children they played with. They had been directly involved. They could see that their understanding of the situation had merit, and that they could trust their own feelings.

The situation was resolved, but I was left with a sobering realization that I was not as democratic as I had thought when it came to my girls. Since then, I understand that, yes, of course, parents need to be mindful of the playmates that their children have and be ready to act if the interaction is not a good one. While it seems so very obvious now, at the time, it was a coming-of-age type of lesson for me. I came face to face with a part of me about which I did not know.

25 *The tone in a person's voice has a meaning that can involve personal safety.*

As readily as I knew it was important for all of us in the family to talk process, express ideas and feelings and ask questions, I also realized that there were infrequent times in life when talking was the last thing that was needed. These times often involved physical safety.

I remember being intrigued watching movies in which I saw someone talking when they were supposed to be quiet. Whether in war trenches or in places where someone bad was stalking the character, the one who talked at the wrong time was usually killed or brought death to all involved. While these scenes were in the movies, it seemed reasonable for the girls to learn that there were times in life when talking was not helpful. At these times, one has to be on the alert for crispness and tone in the leader's voice. Directions are to be followed, without questions or comments—those can be expressed after the danger is past. Although I hoped that Lara and Julie would never need the skill, I thought it important for them to know about it and understand its importance.

By the time Lara was three years old, both girls understood that they were to be aware of tone in a person's voice. I used examples from their lives. If I called Lara from play one day saying in normal tones, "Lara, come in the house now, please."

Then she might rightly say, "Just a minute, Mama, I'm coming. I want to finish playing." Easy. But if she heard the same words with a firmness and urgency in my voice, she was to drop what she was doing and come immediately into the house. Something outside her immediate knowledge was happening. She was to trust that system and be aware of how requests were delivered. Extra loudness, hollering, or screaming would not be the signal; instead, it would be a focused, quiet urgency that meant business. After she and Julie were safely in the house and matters were secure, she would be told what was going on. By quickly acting on her understanding of the tone and urgency, she could help the situation. I further explained that if she were to debate or question the request, she could possibly put all of us in danger. She was to hear the words and act.

We had all talked about situations when it was important to act and not question or talk, but I didn't know how solidly the information took hold. I wondered if the information would be handy for them should they need it. About six months after our talk, Lara, Julie, and I were in the car. As we drove to an intersection, I saw two young men fighting. Several others were running towards the two. I did not know what was going on, but I knew that I wanted us to be safe. I immediately said, "Lara, lock the doors." The tone and urgency was in my voice. Without a word, Lara immediately locked the three doors, lowered herself on the back seat floor, and said, "They're locked." Fear was not in her voice. Then as we drove on, I quietly talked to Lara and Julie about my uneasiness. I told them that I wanted us to be safe while I assessed the situation. I was very grateful that she had acted quickly without questioning and had been helpful.

We experienced several similar times during the next six years. Each time the girls remembered what they knew about that aspect of safety. They also used the same signal when the two of them were together. And later, from a safe distance, assessed their thoughts and instincts.

Years later, when Lara was in college and Julie was at home finishing the last years of high school, she and I had another test. I was working at my desk in the study that overlooked an empty field. It was night and the blinds were not pulled. Julie was in another part of the house doing her homework and Michael was at the University attending to some paperwork. When the phone rang and the caller asked for Michael, I thought he was one of Michael's veterinary students calling about a sick animal. When the caller heard that Michael was not there, he quickly moved into scare tactics. He announced that he could see me and gave me some instructions to follow if I didn't want to be hurt. Thinking he was in the dark empty field outside my study and we were truly in danger, I quickly hung up. At the same time, I called to Julie to get down on the floor. Without question, she dropped to the floor and waited for more information. I crawled to her, told her, and we both crawled upstairs to get to the phone where we could call the police. Julie had remembered clearly what she had been told as a young child. She was not frightened, but she knew what to do. She heard the focused tone and quiet urgency of my voice and she acted immediately. Her quick follow-through allowed me to concentrate on the matter at hand. We discovered that the caller was not in our area and indeed had called many women that night. But, I did not know that at the time of the call. Julie saw that one has to act on the information at hand and analyze it later from a safe distance.

26 *I wanted each of the girls to be comfortable with change, to learn to take change in stride.*

I knew that Lara and Julie's independent lives would have many examples of change, some predictable, like seasonal or developmental, and some that seemed to come without warning. I wanted each of them to be somewhat comfortable with change, to take change in stride, to keep their bearings.

Lara reacted fairly well to change, but I noticed that Julie wasn't so comfortable. She was not balky or devastated, but some change saddened her. Her unease showed when change came quickly and she was expected to adapt. I felt that Michael and I could do her a good service by helping her experience sudden change in a painless way.

Julie was very careful with her environment and liked things to be where she had placed them. Her environment was familiar to her and she liked that. It was something she could depend upon. I decided to use the living room arrangement to help Julie with feelings about a basic change.

One day, while Julie was in upper elementary school, I changed the living room around. Before I moved nearly every piece of furniture, I sketched the way the room looked before Julie left for school that morning. I wanted to respect what I knew about Julie's uneasiness about change. I wanted to give us a return path if we needed it. By the time Lara and Julie arrived home from school, the drastic change was made. Julie was horrified when she saw what had happened. The look on her face said that she had turned her back and look what happened to something she counted on as stable. She cried as she said she didn't like it. I quickly showed her the drawing, and told her I was tired and wondered if we could leave the room the new way for a day or two. If she still didn't like it, we had the drawing and could go back to exactly the way it was before. We examined the drawing together and she could see that nothing was left out. Julie agreed. Three days later, I asked her if we should change back. She said no, she liked it the new way. Her response was treated with dignity and thoughtfulness.

Simple as this approach seems, it gave Julie a way to cope. I would never have disturbed her room, but I could topsy-turvy the family's living room. Several times in her adult life, Julie has commented on that episode. She thinks it helped her adjust to change by letting her see that she had a degree of control over the situation. Julie also tells me that she remembers several times after the living room episode when she toyed with changing her bedroom around. She remembers that I eagerly helped her regardless of how many times we had to squire the furniture around in one day. I don't remember the moves, but Julie tells me that she remembers being intrigued that I never lost my patience as I helped her move the same piece of furniture around until it was "just right." Indeed, yes. I imagine I was so very delighted that a change was being addressed willingly that I stuck with the process for as long, and as often, as Julie was willing.

Since junior high school, both girls have traveled internationally without the family. Each trip, of course, brought quick opportunities to adapt to change as they figured out how to get from one place to another, kept up with their money and passports, kept themselves safe, and had a wonderful time. And, of course, in nearly every part of their lives, change has appeared and been absorbed. In most every change, positive elements were soon apparent to each of the girls.

Julie continues to handle change well. Some change can be sobering and scary, but I've noticed that change doesn't immobilize either of the girls. It is an important attribute, I think.

27 *In life, there are times when someone just needs to act—just do it.*

Procrastination is a wonderful thing sometimes. It gives the feeling that we have control over the situation. Other times, procrastination is apparent to others when we don't want it to be, or it becomes crippling and does us harm. I know that in life there are times when someone just needs to act—just do it. I wanted Lara and Julie to understand that concept.

I remember a story from my own childhood that pointed me in the right direction. One night when I was high school age, my daddy showed me the concept. It was a spring night, Daddy and Mama were in the back part of the house, and my siblings and I were doing homework on the dining room table. It was hot outside and the front room door was open. The screen door was the only barrier and the front porch light was not on. When I heard the doorbell, I went to the door. There was a very large stranger at the door, standing very close to the door and taking up nearly the entire screen frame. He asked for Daddy.

I turned from the door, moving very quickly and turned down the hallway that led to Daddy and Mama's bedroom at the far end of the hallway. In the meantime, Daddy had heard the doorbell and was on his way to the front door. We met midway in the hallway. I was running pretty fast with my long legs.

Daddy saw my efforts, turned around, and started running with me down the hall. When we got to the end of the hallway we had no further place to run. Daddy asked me what was going on. I told him that there was a man to see him. I asked him why he was running. He said that he quickly sized up the situation and felt that the man had to be in the house and was chasing me. He wanted to retreat to a collecting point. The end of the hallway forced us to stop running and assess. We both got the giggles at that point for the inane situation.

Daddy and I had much fun and laughter that night retelling the story to each other. There was such a wonderful philosophical lesson in the episode and Daddy knew the lesson was not lost on me.

I wanted the girls to realize that there comes a time when one needs to act. We started small by mentioning that the grass must be cut, we could wait no longer. Even though we didn't want to do it, the grass was close to seed. Or, we had no more clean dishes; dishes must be washed for it was time to act. The red camper's gas gauge registered empty, it was time to act. Bills were due; it was time to pay. We can wait just so long; then it is time to act. Later there were times when we needed to speak up about an unfairness that could be ignored no longer. Some things just don't disappear. There comes a point when we run out of running-away room, or wait-and-see room. It is time to act, whether we want to or not.

28 *I felt it important that, from a very early age, Lara and Julie understand the vast amount of effort that is required to produce the items we consume.*

I wanted them to know that nearly everything they ever saw had the touch of many people before getting to the stage where we could see it. I thought that understanding this concept would allow them to realize that people are needed for nearly everything. Equally important, I wanted Lara and Julie to realize that their ease through life depended upon the efforts of many people. And, when their work turn came, other people would depend upon Lara and Julie's efforts. People depend upon people, and people are not in isolation, regardless of whether or not they are social. People are important and are to be respected for their contributions within the system. We thought of people as unseen hands behind the product.

We began by talking about the dog food that we bought at the grocery for Shelley. Before our examination, we didn't know how the dog food got to the grocery, we just knew it did, and that we bought it as needed. As we played with the idea, we mentioned the person who placed the order, the one who received the order, the delivery truck, the delivery truck driver, the processor of the food, the designer and producer of the fancy package. We had fun thinking of the many unseen hands that probably touched the process. Each was an important aspect of the final product. Each was needed.

Over time, we played with many different fields and products. We talked about the Montessori teacher whom we all loved, and wondered about all the people who could have been on her path and helped her get to the point where we met her and Lara and Julie became her students. We talked of the theatre production, the post office activities, the Saturday farmers' market, the presidential election, the ballet production, taxes, and the sandals we bought. There was no end to the places and products we could examine from our armchairs. This analyzing process allowed the girls to go beyond the physically obvious.

We also talked about how people might view the product or activity depending upon where they were in its process. The graphic designer of the dog food package was further down the processing line from the farmer who planted the grain, who was down from the delivery person who drove the truck.

We didn't spend a lot of time on this process of understanding for I never wanted things to be heavy-handed. We played with the concept until I knew they understood. It was easy to see why one needed to be respectful to all the people who were involved in the production of an item that we sought or a performance we admired. We would not have the item or the performance without the people who fulfilled the needed roles.

Somewhat along the same line, I enjoyed, in hindsight,

recognizing an activity of the girls' lives that evolved into their careers. When Lara was still in upper elementary school, she would eagerly go outside after storms looking for poor birds that were hurt as the winds tossed them from their nests. Julie would help her look, but it was Lara who patiently tended to the creatures' needs. No bird was too ugly, or too roughed up for her care. Many died, but Lara gave her best to them. Lara's Ph.D. is in immunology. Julie, on the other hand, loved the spring rains as they formed rivulets on the dirt road in front of our house. Where the rest of us saw the spring rains as making driving rough on the dirt road, Julie saw magical places where she could float small things and notice how they moved. Julie could hardly wait to change her school clothes and get out there. She squatted by the rivulets and tested many small, floating things, noticing how blockages worked in the passage-way. While Lara would often play with her, it was Julie's activity and she never tired of it. Julie is finishing a Ph.D. in physical oceanography with a special fondness for ocean currents. Even today, when spring rains come, as I drive on the dirt road in front of our house, I see Julie's imprint, squatting down, float-ing things, and noticing the fluid motions.

The invisible is there for all to see, whether it is the many people who are necessary for producing the item in our hand, or the life blueprint that we each form with our attention and activi-ty. We "see" if we learn to value and give attention to the invisible.

29 *Each family rule seemed necessary, reasonable, fair, and useful for adult life.*

All people have parameters of behavior. Society has expectations of us all. As adults, we encounter many places where we are to behave in a certain way. Many times we are supposed to wait in line until it is our turn; we are to wait until the light is green before we drive on; we are supposed to pay our bills on time; and, we are supposed to remember our best friend's birthday. We are not supposed to growl at or berate the man in the grocery line ahead of us who has forgotten his money. In general, society expects adults to be docile in many of society's circumstances. Society also has expectations for children.

Michael and I rarely told the girls anything more than once. We reasoned that if we got in the habit of repeating things, we were letting the girls know that they did not need to listen the first time. Instead, they could catch the information when it came back around. If they asked for a repeat or for more information, then, of course, it was given.

Consistency was also something that we felt was fair for Lara and Julie. How could they make sense of our family life, if one day one behavior was not allowed and another day, for the parents' convenience, the behavior was allowed? Michael and I had very, very few restrictions for the girls. Those we did have, we had given prior thought to, and each rule seemed necessary, reasonable, fair, and useful for adult life.

As do most parents, we wanted the girls to behave in the grocery store. We wanted no crying, no pleading for items to be purchased, and no bickering between Lara and Julie. We made the statement that if fighting broke out between the two and they would not stop, then we would leave the store. One day as the cart was nearly full, fighting and picking started and wouldn't be silenced. The first warning was a reminder of what they knew. If you don't stop fighting, then we are leaving. Common sense would say that we would not leave, since the shopping was nearly complete and we didn't want to come back. In the bigger picture, it seemed more important for me to deliver on my promise to Lara and Julie than to complete the shopping task for my convenience. I contacted a stocking clerk, told her that we couldn't complete our shopping today, and asked if she would please return the items to the shelves for I needed to take the girls home. We left immediately. Not a word was said in the car. I had learned from my Daddy that children are intelligent and the obvious does not need to be heavy-handedly repeated. Both girls knew why we were on our way home; they did not need to be told.

There was only one more time like this and then it was over. The first reminder was all it took. The fighting often resumed when we got home. But, that was part of the arrangement-fighting was not to occur on outings.

In general, Michael and I thought that any undesirable behavior done the first time was done in ignorance. That we had forgotten to cover that situation. We explained the logic of why we didn't want the behavior and went on about life, much like we would have done had an adult done the same thing. This first-time-done-in-ignorance approach worked very well for us. The girls learned without penalty and parental fussing.

When fussing, fighting or name-calling got out of hand, the instigator was sent to her room. She was to remain there until she felt calm enough to rejoin the family. Many times, I didn't even know who the instigator was, so both girls were sent to their rooms to calm down. Michael and I also went to our room if we were too irritated to deal with a situation. We remained there until we were calmer and could more easily deal with the circumstances. We were lucky in that there were two parents in our household. One could step in when the other was at wit's end. Once when Lara was around two years old, Michael came home and saw that I had had a very long day with Lara. She was constantly talking and asking questions, a very verbal child. As Michael carried Lara out to see the pond, I heard her say, "What's wrong with Mama? Why is she crying?" I was crying because I was worn out. Lara's constant talking that day was like having a hose turned on me full blast all day. Without a partner,

I would have had to seek relief in another spot. Single parents have a rough assignment.

We had very few rules in our family. Neither Michael nor I liked rules for ourselves and we kept our personal rules to a minimum. It seemed only fair that we would have few rules for the girls. Each rule that we did have was one that we thought helped them become functioning adults and helped us deliver the template that guided the child raising.

30

There were times when keeping the focus on the girls made life reasonable for all of us.

Michael and I moved several times in our young lives with Lara and Julie. We were aware that moving is a very complicated event and that, even in the best of circumstances, is a trying one. Our moves were usually long distances. We decided that we would keep our focus on the girls and try to make life as reasonable for them as possible. We usually moved ourselves, so we secured the boxes, packed them, and loaded them onto the rental truck. The girls and I would take one car and Michael would drive the truck. Our longest trip was from California to Maryland.

During the moves, we kept the focus on the girls by not getting fussy with them or each other. And at the end of each driving day, we'd stop a few hours before their normal bed-time. After checking into a motel, we'd find an indoor mall where the girls could walk and run and o-o-o and ah-ah-ah at the store windows. We usually spent an hour letting the girls work off energy and feel free. Before and after the trip, we accomplished in any day only what we could do without com-promising our agreement to make the trip as easy as we could on the girls. Surprisingly, this focus helped Michael and me get through the trips, too. Today, we don't remember the trips as troublesome, but realize that they were quite a feat. The girls remember them fondly.

When we took outings to visit relatives or on holidays, we often drove during the dark hours so the girls could sleep and we would be closer to our destination when they awoke. We pulled down the seats of our red Volkswagen camper to make room for them to lie down. There was a built-in potty-chair. Comics, books, blankets, and pillows were in the back with Lara, Julie, and the dog, Shelley. We sang songs, recited nursery rhymes, and looked for animals along the road. Since we often took trips, and nursery rhymes were so commonly used, the girls had memorized most of a very large book. When Lara entered first grade in Maryland, her teacher told me that Lara knew more nursery rhymes than any child she or the other teachers had ever known.

When I went to school for a master's degree, Michael and I again wanted the focus to be on the girls. Lara was in junior high and Julie was in upper elementary grades. I went to school in the evenings and studied at night after the girls were in bed. The girls did not feel a difference. They knew I was going to school, but my going did not disturb their routines. As they became adults, they said they did not remember my going to school.

Focusing on the girls became a good way for Michael and me to progress through changes in our lives. We weren't martyrs, nor did we think we were giving them undue attention. Focusing on the girls during times of disruption didn't distract from our attention to each other; it just gave us a focus outside ourselves.

31 *The children bought gifts they could afford.*

The girls had collections of inexpensive items. They collected rock specimens, clay marbles, antique postcards of children and holidays, and horse figurines. The cost of each of these items was usually a quarter or less. We went to many rock shows, antique shows, and second-hand stores. The items the girls collected were some of the most inexpensive things in any of the places. We liked that each daughter could afford to buy a present for the other when the occasion arose. The girls got small amounts of money for doing extra household jobs, and sometimes a gift of money from a friend or family member. They were very careful with their money and it lasted them a long time.

I developed a collection that the girls could afford, too. I began a collection of small colorful tins. At this time, each tin was less than fifty cents. The girls delighted in pooling their money to buy something for me. The collection is quite extensive now and is on display in the living room. Michael enjoyed small, used, wind-up toys, the prices of which were also well within the girls' combined resources.

Each of our collections involved things that contained history. We enjoyed looking at the tins, arranging the pretty rock collections, and admiring the beautiful postcards and reading the messages on the back.

We frequented garage sales and found many treasures. I remember one time the girls bought me a bamboo back scratcher at a garage sale for a quarter. Lara and Julie split the cost, cleaned it carefully to remove the body cells from the previous owner, wrapped it, and presented it to me on my birthday. I was absolutely delighted and pronounced it one of the finest birthday presents I had ever received. They saw that I used it many times and that I made sure it was in my suitcase when I traveled.

None of us ever had to pretend that we liked a present since it was obvious that the inexpensive item went into a collection that we were cultivating. We all gave attention to each other's collections. We recognized when we saw something at a garage sale that was new to one of our collections. It was a good feeling for all of us.

32 *Panic is an awful feeling.*

Not only are we scared, but we also have a bad feeling of being out of control in a situation without assurance that help will come in time.

One day when the girls were still very young, all four of us were in an airplane museum enjoying the pictures and models of many decades of planes. It was a wonderful outing for the history of planes was an interesting subject to us. The museum was not crowded and there was lots of space around the displays so the girls were free to wander from us more than usual as they admired the exhibits. It was a winter day so we each had coats and hats with us. Michael and I were carrying the girl's navy coats. Julie had tucked her hat inside her coat sleeve, but Lara had kept hers. The knit hat had a loop at the top and Lara stuck her finger into the hat loop to easily keep up with it. As she and Julie moved through the exhibits, she twirled the hat that was hanging on her finger. We were all four in the same very large exhibit hall and Michael and I easily had an eye on the girls as we all enjoyed the wonderful outing.

Suddenly we heard both girls crying. When we got to them, their little faces were quite red from crying and they looked scared. Lara held up her finger, which was very blue. Her twirling had twisted the hat's loop around her finger until it was clearly digging in and cutting off blood. All Lara could think about was that she was in pain and the pain was getting worse by the minute. She didn't know how to help herself and in her imagination, the situation looked very bleak. Perhaps she would lose a finger. Julie took her cue from her older sister. Julie saw the finger getting increasingly blue and saw Lara crying and very concerned. Julie knew that if it was serious enough for Lara to be so concerned, then surely Julie needed to be concerned, too. The more scared they became, the more they cried. I think they drew scared energy from each other by this time. Lara's face had a desperate look to it.

We released the hat's grip on Lara's finger by reversing its course. We took the girls to a nearby resting area, comforted them, and heard the details. Then I asked Lara how she felt when she realized she was in trouble. Lara said that she felt awful and sick at her stomach and helpless. I reminded her that she had the information that she needed to help herself. As she began to feel pain in her finger, she could assess the situation and see that the hat loop was involved in the problem. Further, she would know that her twirling was making the loop smaller. If the loop was getting smaller and hurting, then she needed to think how to stop the getting smaller. Go the opposite way; undo the twisting. It could be similar to knots in hair ribbons and Lara knew how to get those out.

Lara was very surprised to hear that she could have easily taken care of the situation. As she realized the truth of what I told her, she was bewildered that she had forgotten what she knew. I explained to her that she had just experienced panic. We talked about how it had started to build in her and how she might be able to recognize the feeling if it were to ever come again. If she felt the feeling again, she could think carefully and quickly about what she knew about the situation. It was important to do this while still calm, since she now knew how quickly the feeling of panic could take over. Julie listened carefully to our talk, for she had been quite actively caught up in the situation.

As we talked, I reminded Lara and Julie of a time when Lara had assessed an uneasy situation wonderfully well. She had not panicked. Lara was about three and a half years old and Julie was around two.

Both girls had cribs in the same room at the end of the hallway. One night, when Michael was out of town, the girls were asleep and I was reading in the living room. They had been asleep for a couple of hours when I heard Lara call out to me. "Mama, there is a big, big bird flying around in here!" There was only wonderment in her voice, for she was simply transferring information to me. Such an outlandish statement! I knew that the statement was so very outlandish that it surely was true. I hurried down the hallway, wondering what I would find in their bedroom. I kept concentrating on the words: big, bird. Just as I got to the door, something very large swooped by me and down the hall to the living room. As I moved into the bedroom, here came the big bird again.

I noticed that the bird was not hitting anything, not bumping into anything in the dark.

I realized that the big, big bird had to be a bat and that it was using its sonar to navigate.

How strange. I was fascinated, but along with the sonar information, I had other thoughts swirling in my head. How it had come into the house was a minor question when measured against the thought of a bite and rabies.

I turned on the light, and calmly told the girls what the big, big bird was. I got them out of bed and we walked down the hallway. The bat was in the kitchen area. I turned the bright kitchen light on and the bat immediately hung upside down at the top of a cabinet. The light had stopped the bat. The girls and I examined it from a short distance while I was thinking about how to get the bat out of the house. I called the police who said I should call the fire station. Two kind firemen came with heavy gloves and took the bat away. In that week's local paper was a small notice that the fire station had made a run to the Pullen's home to remove a bat.

Lara had confronted an unknown and treated it with logic. She knew that birds fly and they can come in several sizes. She didn't stop to wonder at that point how it got in. She had just been awakened by the swishing sound and wanted to transfer information to me. She had not cried or panicked. She had used information that she had to alleviate the situation. She had trusted and remembered what she knew.

Although the girls have been scared plenty of times as they were growing up, each time they have fairly quickly assessed the situation rather than panic.

33 *Parents have aspects to their lives other than parenthood.*

Being a parent takes immense energy and attention. It is not good if a parent thinks that his life is being robbed of wonderful things because of what he is giving to the child. A resentment can set in that is not good for either the parent or the child. Resentment can color interactions between child and parent.

There is no doubt that Michael and I gave a wonderful amount of attention and energy to the girls during their forming years. That was our conscious choice, our responsibility to help the girls grow. But throughout those early years, Michael and I never forgot that we "were here first." I was concerned that if the girls thoughts that our lives were consumed by them, they might decide that parenting is too demanding and would decide not to have children of their own. Though Lara and Julie certainly might decide not to have children, I wanted their decisions to be based on their own choices not on a life deficiency that they noticed in Michael and me. We needed to take care of ourselves first. We could also be better parents if we gave attention to ourselves. That approach seemed fair and fair play was one of the items on the template. We needed to live what we talked about and valued.

The girls had very early bedtimes. Not only did Michael

and I think that large amounts of evening sleep was good for growing children, but we also wanted some time alone together.

Lara and Julie knew that Michael and I were not just parents to them. We each had other aspects to our lives. Michael and I knew about Lara and Julie's daily play, heard their dreams, and discussed issues in their lives. It seemed reasonable and fair that Lara and Julie would know Michael's and my work, dreams, and issues. We were all together in the family and it seemed fair to expect us to be concerned and involved in aspects of each other's lives and growth. There was not a separation between adult work life and family life; and we never hesitated to discuss either. The talking occurred during ordinary activities like cooking meals or clearing the dishes from the table.

Before Lara began first grade, both girls knew where Michael worked, the names of people he worked with, and some of his work dreams. Later, when I began working in a school district, they knew my activities, concerns, and dreams.

Some families elect to not speak of work in the home, to not "bring work home." Wonderful experiences happen regularly to people outside the walls of home. If children do not frequently hear of parents' activities outside of home, parents may not frequently hear of the child's activities outside of home. School is the child's work for at least twelve years.

Nearly all parents like it when the child easily tells of her school life. Parents can lead the way by early letting the child hear of their work. How the parent speaks of work may be reflected later in how the child speaks and thinks of his work at school.

It's difficult to be supportive of family members if you don't know their work and some of their dreams and plans for themselves. And, it helps family members to talk out loud of their plans. By talking and answering questions, frustrations can sometimes lessen and dreams and plans can become more real.

34 *Parents' comments help form standards.*

Young children take their cues from their parents about what is good, what is not so good, what is or is not acceptable, and what is valued in the family. Michael and I chose to transfer this family knowledge through positive comments. We gave many comments in the form of feedback to the girls. The feedback almost always carried specific examples with it. It was not enough to just say that something was done well. We felt it was important for us to tell the girls why we felt that something was good, to talk of the details.

We wanted Lara and Julie to tell us the details of a drawing or a project. We liked them to analyze their projects and tell us about the development and choices they made as they designed and created. We asked to hear about the process of the activity. It became clear to Michael and me that much of the richness of a drawing or an activity lay in our hearing about the individual choices that our daughter had made.

In high school, Julie completed an assigned project in which she explained existentialism. She posed friends for individual slides and told them to just look natural and somewhat blank-to just "be." Then she played *2001: A Space Odyssey* music as background. With only the soaring music to accompany the somber slides, the three-minute project was fascinating. The richness was most revealed, however, when Julie explained to us why she had selected black and white film; why she had selected a small amount of headroom as she shot the slides; why she had selected that particular music; and why she thought that the project said so much about existentialism. Teachers and other adults don't have the time to inquire of, and listen to, the details of what lies behind every pupil's piece of work. As parents, we can take the time. When a child explains a project, parents hear about the child's behind-the-scenes thoughts, and the child is pleased to have the opportunity to explain that there is more to the project than what one sees.

This same child often grows up to be an adult who will inquire about the details of a friend's work. And, we all know how wonderful that is. I suspect that the tendency can be cultivated in childhood.

After I heard the details of the choices that Lara had made in designing a particular project, then I could comment with clarity on the cleverness of her thinking. As she grew older, when I commented on one of her current projects, I was reminded of something she had created before. She and I both liked that I could point out another time when she showed equally fine thinking. She was pleased that I had remembered, and I was pleased that I could reinforce that she had a fine skill or trait that frequently showed. I was letting Lara know that I was paying attention and valuing her work/play.

I frequently commented privately to Lara and Julie of

specific examples where I saw that they were kind, caring, very clever, very intelligent, quick thinking, or very witty. Comments help form standards. If I quietly talked of a time when Julie was so very kind, then I noticed that the behavior became common for her. If I didn't give a specific example, then the words seemed like just that-words with no backing. They were only a parent's biased words. However, if I had specifics, they knew that I was analyzing and paying attention to a situation, just as I expected them to do. Comments helped Lara and Julie see good and value in themselves as they interacted with, and produced within, their environments.

35 *Wishes can carry more than the obvious.*

When we lived in Davis, California, we saw many cute small
rabbits each spring. They were so very cuddly, perfect to dress
up and play with and read to. Any of them would make a fine
real life playmate. And, Lara and Julie wanted one so very much.

One day, a veterinarian colleague told Michael that he had
a small rabbit and wondered if Michael would like it for Lara
and Julie. The girls were absolutely delighted. They named him
Trixie. Trixie's fur was a pretty light brown; he was small, and
didn't mind wearing a hat and being read to. He also liked to
be taken on tricycle rides and liked to play in the small wading
pool with the girls. His home was an open cage in the enclosed
patio off the living room.

It wasn't long before Trixie became a handful. He had a
wary look, but we thought perhaps all rabbits have a wary look
as they get older. He developed increasingly powerful hind
legs. He could push off from the girls and nearly knock them
down in the process, often seriously scratching their arms.

Trixie grew at an alarming rate until he was very long,
powerful, and big. He certainly was no longer fun to play with.
Most rabbits we had seen aged differently-their size remained
relatively small; they just got less active, a little dull. Trixie was
very active and certainly not dull. At night, we secured the
door to his cage and we could hear him thrashing around the

cage, over and over, propelling himself onto all six sides. Lara and Julie became afraid of him. Michael and I worried that Trixie would scratch the girls' faces.

During this time, Michael discovered that Trixie was a Himalayan Jack Rabbit that naturally grew to very large proportions and, furthermore, that Trixie was in mating form. We never discovered how we got a Himalayan Jack Rabbit, but he was a sight to behold and to hear at night. We told the girls that Trixie was developing the way he was supposed to because he was a Himalayan Jack Rabbit. We also told them that most rabbits did not grow to be that large. We talked about how we had wished for a cute little rabbit and how our wish grew into something that we didn't want. He wasn't anything like what we had wished for.

Later, when Lara and Julie read about the *Iliad*, they likened Trixie to the Trojan Horse. After the Himalayan Jack Rabbit experience, wishes were analyzed in a different fashion than they would have been if Trixie had not appeared on the scene. Wishes can carry more than the obvious. It is useful to extend the implication of wishes while they are still in the talking and planning stages in order to avoid a Himalayan Jack Rabbit.

Conclusion

In raising Lara and Julie, our two children, Michael and I were respectful of them and of ourselves. Throughout the parenting process, we were mindful of the template that expressed the skills and attributes that we wanted for our adult daughters.

The template required conscious choices from Michael and me as we guided them to adulthood. Today we clearly see the template expressed in both of our daughters.

There is hardly a more fascinating project than parenthood. You are responsible for not only physically creating the baby, but for creating the early foundation that the child will use to form the adult.

You will make your impression upon your child whether you have specific intentions or not. You'll do this by role modeling, by where you give attention, by the words you use, and by the aspects of life you value. Your child will constantly observe you and learn from you, just as you did with your parents. You'll make choices of how you impress your child whether you have intentions or not. By being thoughtful ahead of time, you will make purposeful choices in how you raise your child.

Being a parent is not easy work; it is responsible work, full of choices at nearly every step of the way, just as it was for your parents and their parents before them. By being purposeful and respectful in your choices, you will know why you are making the steps in the way that you are. It will give you a sense of comfort as you move through a very insecure path- the path of parenthood.

Each of us has received a foundation from our parents. Then, from adulthood to the end of our lives, we are responsible for all adjustments, enhancements, and changes that are made on the foundation. By being respectful and observant of ourselves, and making conscious choices, we move forward in wise growth.

Thank you

My thanks and special love to Michael, Lara, and Julie who are always there for me in the very important ways that count.

My thanks and love to my sisters Gayle Davis and Nan Ternes who always make me feel special and supported.

My thanks and special gratitude to Joan Wolf, Pam Zimba, and Ben Lewis who read the early drafts of the first chapters of the book and encouraged me down the path.

My thanks and amazement to Dorie McClelland for the professional talent and magical taste that she brought to the synergy that produced this book.

My thanks and wonderment to my people who have overseen this book and who, with care, oversee my experiences and interactions.

My thanks and delight to my mama and daddy who laid my foundation.

Jeanie Davis Pullen

is an educator, consultant, and speaker with an advanced degree in gifted education. She is a high school teacher and also teaches graduate courses at the university level. For over thirteen years, Jeanie has been the director of a large summer institute for gifted children in the Minneapolis/St. Paul area. As a teacher and administrator, she has encouraged hundreds of people to see that life is rich with possibilities and choices. As a speaker, Jeanie is known for her conversational delivery of reflective wisdom and common sense.

Three additional books for adults are
in preparation by the author.

Life Teachings: Communicating
Life Teachings: Preparing for Work
Life Teachings: Leadership